PERCEPTION AND COMMUNICATION IN INTERCULTURAL SPACES

Lily A. Arasaratnam

University Press of America,® Inc.
Lanham · Boulder · New York · Toronto · Plymouth, UK

Copyright © 2011 by
University Press of America,® Inc.
4501 Forbes Boulevard
Suite 200
Lanham, Maryland 20706
UPA Acquisitions Department (301) 459-3366

Estover Road
Plymouth PL6 7PY
United Kingdom

Library of Congress Control Number: 2010942905
ISBN: 978-0-7618-5459-3 (paperback : alk. paper)
eISBN: 978-0-7618-5460-9

To my parents, who gave me the opportunity and freedom to travel the world and experience new cultures.

TABLE OF CONTENTS

PREFACE

Someone once asked me, "Is there a difference between intercultural communication competence and communication competence in general? Wouldn't someone who is a competent communicator be competent regardless of context?" I have given these questions a great deal of thought over the years. But I keep arriving at the same answer: yes, there are indeed skills and qualities that competent communicators (intercultural or otherwise) possess—but intercultural communication *is* different from other forms of communication because of the added measure of complexities brought on by cultural differences. In other words, a person who is a competent communicator in an American corporate boardroom may not necessarily be competent in communicating with locals in a business meeting in Mumbai. A competent intercultural communicator possesses certain abilities beyond the abilities of a communicator who is competent in a specific cultural context. These abilities enable the competent intercultural communicator to not only recognise differences in context but also be attuned to the subtle nuances that are characteristic of *intercultural spaces*.

In most industrialised nations it is not uncommon for a person to be born in one country, educated in another, and perhaps be employed in yet another. Depending on the extent to which the person assimilates each of those country's cultural norms, she or he may have a unique cultural identity that is hard to categorise.

When does such an individual participate in intercultural communication (as opposed to interpersonal communication)? Perhaps the determining factor is when cultural differences between the relevant individuals affect the communication exchange in ways which would have been insignificant had those differences not existed. I see these particular communication interactions as occurring in *intercultural spaces*. These are not spaces in the physical sense of the word. They are instead symbolic markers of these particular types of communication exchanges. In other words, intercultural communication occurs in intercultural spaces. An intercultural space is therefore a symbolic representation of an instance when communication between individuals is affected by cultural differences in a way that would not have been noteworthy in the absence of these differences.

A competent intercultural communicator is someone who is conversant in navigating communication in intercultural spaces. Admittedly, intercultural communication competence is more complex than what is captured in this single sentence. In order to engage in a meaningful discussion of intercultural communication in today's multicultural societies, however, it is necessary to begin with a simple premise in which the complexities of today's reality can be captured. Once we identify intercultural communication as communication that unfolds in intercultural spaces, we are then in a position to discuss the rich and complex nature of intercultural spaces. It is in this discussion that we will engage, in this book.

In the presence of multiple texts and resources in intercultural communication, there is no need for yet another book which rehashes what has already been eloquently and comprehensively written by others. Instead, I see this book as a synthesis of ideas that will further our understanding of communication in intercultural spaces. The introductory chapter further details the nature and contents of this book.

Acknowledgment

Many people's friendship and encouragement has sustained me throughout this book project. If I were to name all of them, I imagine that the acknowledgement section would rival the rest of the book in length. I am grateful for the support of my family, friends, and mentors who have not only cheered me on throughout my academic career but also helped me with this particular book project in practical ways such as proofreading and providing helpful feedback. I am indebted to all of them for their generosity.

I must, however, give special thanks to three gentlemen with whom I have shared friendship since the uniquely formative years of university: Dr. Zim Okoli, whose constructive feedback greatly improved my writing, Dr. Chris Glover whose enthusiastic responses to my short stories was a refreshing source of encouragement, and the late Dr. Yeh Wei Kho who foresaw this book, years before it was written. Thank you.

INTRODUCTION

We live in interesting times. On the one hand, there is dynamic fusion of cultures and ideas even to the point that in many contexts it is impossible to identify discrete cultural identities as we once did. On the other hand, we are faced with violence and strife instigated by the rigid adherence to cultural identities where one is defined by the exclusion of the *other*. As recently as a few decades ago it may have been hard to imagine that both of these extremes would exist simultaneously at this point in history. But they do. In one reality, the defining and redefining of cultural identity happens at both the individual level as well as the societal level, propelled by globalisation, migration, and intercultural dialogue. In another reality, friction brews as some continue to hold on to specific cultural identities and ways of life even at times to the point of instigating hostilities against those who are perceived as a threat to this goal. Given cultural identity in of itself is a fluid entity, one has to wonder whether any measures taken to ensure the "unpolluted" retention of a particular cultural identity are inherently futile.

In the Westernised technologically progressive societies, globalisation and the melding of cultural groups are part of everyday reality. Much research, thought, and discussion are invested on grabbling with a rapidly changing world in which it is increasingly difficult to categorise persons into distinct cultures. The assumptions under which research in intercultural communication used to operate are fast becoming obsolete. With the advent of social media, communicating with people from across the world is no longer limited to the parameters of travel and telephone conversations.

It is easy for someone who lives in such a Westernised, culturally diverse society to assume that the world is becoming the global village of McLuhan's (1964) vision. Perhaps we may even begin to envision a time in the not-too-distant future where discrete cultures as we know them will cease to exist. This is, however, a limited view of reality.

Even though cultural diversity is normative in economically advanced societies, there are many parts of the world, particularly in developing countries, where cultural homogeneity is still very much the norm. International travel and access to information technologies are still limited to those who have the means to afford these. To a significant majority, the reality remains one of day to day survival and the search for the next meal.

As I begin writing about intercultural communication, I want to acknowledge the reality of this latter group of people because it is easy to get carried away with the notion that cultural heterogeneity and the contemplation of its consequences is commonplace worldwide, when that is not the case. Those of us who have the privilege of being further along on Maslow's (1943) hierarchy of needs have the luxury of reflecting on our cultural identity and how we relate to others who do not share it. But those who live in conditions where their physiological needs have not yet been met are not able to contemplate matters beyond those immediate needs. Therefore it must be acknowledged that this discussion of intercultural communication is based on, and biased by, the perspective of those few of us who have the ability to contribute to it. I too am one such individual, and I write from the perspective of the world with which I am most familiar—the culturally heterogeneous, technologically advanced, economically affluent one.

One of the challenges that today's researcher faces is the very nature of intercultural communication as defined by researchers at the onset of this field of study. The world (or at least parts of it) is a far more culturally integrated place than it was at the time of the early intercultural researchers. Therefore it is necessary to re-address what we mean by intercultural communication before engaging in a discussion of this subject.

Researchers in communication generally agree that intercultural communication is interpersonal communication between individuals from different cultures (Gudykunst, 2002). Culture, in turn, can be conceptualised as a collective where norms, traditions, rituals, and values are shared. But when does an interpersonal exchange become intercultural communication? Does it depend on differences in national culture? Differences in ethnicity? Where exactly is the line of demarcation beyond which interpersonal communication becomes intercultural communication? Globalisation and migration patterns make it increasingly difficult to answer this question.

When we think of intercultural communication as communication that unfolds in intercultural spaces, however, the answer to this question becomes clearer.

Often in intercultural spaces, one views the other as the *other*, someone whose worldview, at least in some aspects, is distinctly different from one's own. The *other* is not necessarily an object of hostility or dubiousness, but an entity with a measure of inherent ambiguity.

The means to communicate with the *other* and the means to find out about the *other* have never been as accessible as they are today. Yet communication and the eventual acquisition of knowledge do not seem to unilaterally contribute to global dialogue and harmonious co-existence of cultures. We already know the reasons for this; if we only pause to consider them. Whether we would choose to act on changing the status quo, however, is an entirely different matter.

The answers to the question of why increased knowledge of and exposure to other cultures do not seamlessly lead to enhanced intercultural relations lie in a variety of places such as our perceptual processes, the way in which we construct our social reality, and our existential fears, to name a few. These, along with theories and frameworks that help us to understand intercultural communication, will be explored in this book.

About This Book

We live in a time where a waiting period of ten minutes is far too long (ever waited ten minutes to download something from the Internet?). As much as technological advancements have facilitated expediency in everyday tasks, we seem to have filled the extra time presumably created by technological efficiency with more things that require our attention. Meta-reflection is arguably low on the list of priorities in such an environment. But unless we pause to consider the factors that under gird the social phenomena we observe today, we may realise in retrospect that we have paid too high a price for expediency. One of the purposes of this book is to engage in this meta-reflection of culture, cognition, and communication.

A glance at the shelves of any popular bookstore reveals our obsession with quick solutions. Five minute meals, ten steps to being a great leader, flat abs guaranteed in six easy moves, or seven keys to effective communication. Perhaps a book on "Five steps to figuring out your cultural identity" or "Ten secrets to intercultural competence" might be a much more lucrative venture. Alas, this is not such a book. Rather, the purpose of this book is to discuss the *what* and the *why* of intercultural issues in the hope that the readers can arrive at the *how* by adapting their understanding to suit their own contexts—given the *how* is as varied as the contexts in which they may find themselves.

The discussion in this book includes the theoretical frameworks prevalent in intercultural literature as well as reflections on the practical applications of these frameworks—Chapters 1 through 5 encompass this content. These chapters also contain illustrative elements such as mini case studies and "conversation breaks" in which key issues are highlighted in conversations between two fictitious characters, Chris and Anusha, who appear throughout the book. Though the book is aimed at students of intercultural communication, its contents are relevant to anyone who wishes to equip themselves with better understanding of cultural influences on communication. Hence the mini case studies and conversation breaks are designed for the purpose of introducing some of the theoretical concepts to readers who may be new to the study of intercultural communication.

Chapter 6 does not resemble the other chapters. There is a specific reason for this. In my experience, communication in intercultural spaces happens organically, especially in today's multicultural societies. The subject cannot be studied and understood fully in a de-contextualised, simulated way. Though the study of critical incidents is useful in poignantly highlighting key issues for discussion, in my own journey I have learned the most important lessons in intercultural communication through everyday narratives and experiences in intercultural spaces. Those of us who have had the opportunity to travel to different countries and cultures have experienced homesickness, confusion, desperation, rejection, regret, and loneliness, along with delight, joy, excitement, friendship, novelty, curiosity, and incredulity. Though these are not experiences that are unique to intercultural spaces, they are often heightened in such contexts. Part of the learning process in better understanding intercultural communication, in my opinion, is to experience these heightened emotions as they occur in everyday intercultural encounters.

Given not everyone has the opportunity to experience communication in intercultural spaces firsthand, the next best thing is to experience it vicariously. To this end, Chapter 6 consists of several short stories that capture communication in everyday intercultural spaces. Though the stories themselves can be enjoyed for the reader's pleasure, as a pedagogical (or more precisely, andragogical) strategy, each story is succeeded by a section in which a main character is "interviewed" by me, the author. In these interviews, key concepts are highlighted and explicit connections are made between these concepts and the ideas discussed in preceding chapters. It is my hope that the stories will serve to subtly educate, as real-life experiences do.

This book is hence intended to educate, provoke, inspire, and contribute to the ongoing discussion of intercultural communication.

Chapter One
COMMUNICATION AND SOCIAL COGNITION

Being an avid fan of science fiction, I spent a considerable amount of time watching the television show *Stargate SG1* (Cooper & Wood, 2002) as a university student. In one episode there is a conversation between the male protagonist, Jack O'Neill, and his alien teammate, Teal'c. In this conversation, Teal'c tries to convince O'Neill that O'Neill should consider Jonas, another alien, as a possible member of their team. O'Neill responds by looking at Teal'c with incredulity and says, "But he's an *a . . . lien.*" Realisation dawns on O'Neill as he finishes his sentence that he was, in fact, in conversation with an alien, though Teal'c had been on the team for a long time. In O'Neill's mind Teal'c was no longer an outsider; he was just as valuable and familiar to him as the other human members of his team. However, Jonas, being new to the group, was very much an alien, despite the fact that Jonas' physical appearance was more "human" than that of Teal'c. As this example illustrates, our perceptions of familiarity, and our allegiance to whom we perceive as our "own kind," are factors of everyday social cognitive processes that influence our decisions in a significant way (Stephan & Stephan, 2002).

The role of perceptual processes in influencing our understanding of what is familiar and what is alien cannot be overstated. Cultural traditions, such as our values and beliefs, create cognitive traditions of which we are not necessarily always cognizant. By cognitive traditions I mean patterns of perception, recognition, and thought that influence everyday decisions. Cognitive sociologist Zerubavel (1997) calls them *cognitive norms*. These are learnt, and they influence how we perceive something as important or relevant.

Every day we make decisions of *selection* and *interpretation* when choosing which stimuli are relevant at any given moment in time. It is clear that cultural traditions influence and perhaps even dictate how this selection and interpretation happen. For example, in a Western context, if a man wants to find out whether a woman is married, he would look for a strategically placed ring on her left hand. If the man is, on the other hand, from a Hindu culture, he would look at the woman's neck instead, to see whether she is wearing a marriage necklace. The particular piece of jewellery in each case is selected as relevant and then interpreted as an important clue as to the lady's marital status. As is evident from this example, the extent to which our attention is drawn to a particular stimulus is greatly influenced by our culture.

Another example to which most of us can relate is the matter of recognising one's skin colour. When we first see a person, the colour of his/her skin is something we notice straight away. Even though there are many other physical attributes that are just as easily recognisable on first glance such as the person's height, weight, or shape of forehead, somehow we notice skin colour. We note whether the person is black, white, brown, or any other variation that is significant to us, and then assign a meaning as to where that person fits in our social landscape. Years of history and social indoctrination have taught us that skin colour is an important stimulus to which we must pay attention—and so we do.

Once we take note of a particular stimulus, we proceed to place it in an appropriate category in our mental filing system. In the example of skin colour, we may decide either that the person belongs to our ingroup or that the person is someone who should be categorised as a member of an outgroup. In this chapter, social cognitive processes, and their relevance to intercultural communication, are discussed.

Schemata

Our perception is influenced by our schemata, which are cognitive structures with which we understand our environment. Schemata enable us to recognise and organise everyday stimuli we encounter in our environment, without having to relearn them over and over again. In other words, we are not disconcerted by traffic every time we walk out the door because, from past experiences, we know what a car is and, when we see one, recognise it as a familiar mode of transportation. If, on the other hand, we see a flying car when we step out of the door, that might be quite disconcerting because our schematic framework for a car does not (at least at the present time!) include flying.

An example of a schematic structure is a *prototype*. A prototype is an ideal representation of an object, person, or event. For example, the prototype for a chair could be a form that has four legs, a seat, and a back. So whenever you encounter an object which has these characteristics, you are likely to identify it as a chair. Even though there are variations in the way chairs are designed, they seem to bear enough resemblance to the prototype of a chair such that one can recognise them to be chairs. We recognise things, places, and even events by comparing our encounters to the prototypes in our mind. This is why we do not have to relearn every aspect of our environment on a daily basis.

As one might imagine, prototypes are influenced by culture. For example, the prototype for a beautiful woman in a contemporary Westernised culture is slender, toned, perhaps with flowing shinny hair, not too tall, not too short. We know this because we see such women depicted in magazines, runways, and movies as ideal forms of beauty. In many African cultures on the other hand, the prototypical beauty is voluptuous and full-figured. The slender form of the Western "beauty" would not be considered appealing in such a cultural context. Our perception is therefore influenced by the prototypes to which our culture has predisposed us.

A *script* is another example of a schematic structure. A script is a sequence of events that one is supposed to experience/expect in a particular context. For example, a script for "the first day of class" in a university might look like this: the professor walks in, introduces herself to the class, checks the class roster, hands out the course outline and reading lists, discusses the expectations of the class, answers questions, and then delivers a general introductory lecture on the relevant topic. We learn scripts based on our past experiences and through the collective memory of the society in which we operate. Though there may be slight variations in specific scripts, generally speaking, a student who has previously experienced "first day of class" in a university is familiar with this script and knows what to expect in a "first day of class" situation. Knowing what we are supposed to expect in a particular situation brings a level of comfort, as there is minimal room for ambiguity.

Scripts are culturally constructed as well. A good example of cultural differences in scripts is that of scripts for weddings. Each culture has its unique set of rituals and sequences that are part of a wedding ceremony, and any deviation from that script could be considered rebellious, innovative, or even scandalous. Like prototypes, scripts also colour the way we see the world, influencing what we consider as "normal" and what we perceive as strange.

Schemata not only help us to understand and interact with our environment by providing us with conceptual frameworks with which to navigate the complexity of our world, but also help us to categorise and process information in a way we can manage. In the example of the *Stargate* episode discussed earlier, we can surmise that O'Neill's schema of an alien consisted of someone with whom he was unfamiliar—not someone who looked alien in appearance. Hence Teal'c, having been part of the team for a long time, did not belong in the category of "alien" while Jonas, though very much human in appearance, did— because Jonas was relationally unfamiliar to O'Neill. As the example illustrates, our schemata are shaped by our personal experiences and preferences as well as the socio-cultural context in which we are raised.

Horace Miner (1956) writes about a tribe of people he encountered somewhere on the North American continent. According to Miner this tribe, called the *Nacirema*, had strange customs and rituals. Each household had shrines in which rituals and ceremonies were conducted on a daily basis, particularly to combat the human body's natural propensity to debility as the tribal people believed. Every shrine had a charm box in which the tribal people kept the magical materials and potions necessary for some of these rituals. Miner provides further information about these customs:

> The charm is not disposed of after it has served its purpose, but is placed in the charmbox of the household shrine. As these magical materials are specific for certain ills, and the real or imagined maladies of the people are many, the charm-box is usually full to overflowing. The magical packets are so numerous that people forget what their purposes were and fear to use them again. While the natives are very vague on this point, we can only assume that the idea in retaining all the old magical materials is that their presence in the charm-box, before which the body rituals are conducted, will in some way protect the worshipper (p. 504).

The ways of the *Nacirema* are arguably quite strange to someone whose schematic frameworks are influenced by a Westernised view of the world. However, there are certain patterns of familiarity that become obvious upon a closer look at Miner's description. Rewording the above portion of Miner's article by substituting seemingly strange concepts with more familiar ones, the paragraph might read something like this:

> The medicine is not disposed of after it has served its purpose but is placed in the first aid kit of the household bathroom. As these tablets are specific for certain ailments, and the real or imagined symptoms of the people are many, the first aid kit is usually full to overflowing. The various tablets and medicines are so numerous that people forget what their purposes were and fear to use them again. While the locals are very vague on this point, we can only assume that the idea in retaining all the expired medicines is that their presence in the first aid kit, before which the daily rituals of brushing teeth, washing up, etc. are conducted, will in some way protect the person.

As is evident from the second reading of the text, our schematic frameworks influence how we recognise something as familiar or not and inform our orientation to what we perceive as "normal." Miner was in fact not describing a remote strange tribe, but instead delineating the ways of the North American people (as the astute person might note, *Nacirema* is American spelt backwards). Understanding this role of schemata in influencing our perception of normality is essential to understanding how our cultural preferences may debilitate our ability to engage someone else's perspective, particularly in intercultural interactions.

Categorisation

We live in a world of categories. The globe is structured into countries, borders, cities, territories, etc. Having decided how the world should be structured, we have assigned meaning to these structures. We place great emphasis on one's membership to a particular group of people. A significant part of our identity is derived from our national affiliation and the collective historic memory we share with others who share our nationality. We feel insulted when someone speaks derogatively about this symbolic entity called our "country" and derive pride when fellow countrymen and women obtain accolades in international sporting events (though we personally had little to do with their success!).

Historic events notwithstanding, the arbitrary nature of national boundaries is evident when you stand at the border of two countries. Somehow crossing the few metres between one and the other makes you transition from being an insider to an outsider. On one side of the line you are expected to adhere to one set of laws while on the other side of the line an entirely different set of laws apply.

Nationalities, territories, and cultural groups are symbolic distinctions we have created for our own functional purposes. We have participated in these social structures as far back as our historic memory would allow such that we may no longer be capable of recognising our part in the very creation of these structures. Berger and Lukman (1966) caution us that, unless we are careful, we are likely to externalise and objectify social structures, thus forgetting our role in creating them in the first place. The fact remains, at the most basic level, the way in which our world is conceptually divided into countries and continents is a form of categorisation – not unlike the process of categorisation in which we engage every day on a regular basis.

We deal with the enormity of an infinitely complex world by categorising it into manageable cognitive structures. For example, we have broad categories to identify random objects as "furniture," "garden tools," "office supplies," etc. These categories are culturally influenced as well, as illustrated in the example of a snake belonging to the category of "pests" in one culture, "pets" in another, and "food" in yet another. When we encounter a new stimulus, there is a neurological search to find a category in which it fits. Similarly, when we encounter a new person we try to fit the person in a category in order to have a basis from which to evaluate or interact with that person.

When we see a new person, we most probably notice his or her sex (presumably based on the person's attire, stature, and other physiological features we have come to associate with a man or woman); assuming the person is a woman, we may take notice of other things such as the colour of her skin and hair. If she is dressed in a manner which we associate with a certain age group, we may gauge her age accordingly. Processing the information we gather about her colouring, we determine her ethnicity—using pre-existing frameworks that correspond to our understanding of ethnic groups. Once these factors are established, we may have feelings of affiliation or adversity toward the woman based on our orientation to the sex, age, ethnic group (and perhaps even social class) with which we associate her. Arguably, there are several points in this process where one can make an error in judgment. Regardless, we navigate our world every day in this manner—by selecting a piece of information, interpreting it, and then categorising it.

Even if we encounter a person in a context in which we do not foresee an imminent interaction, we still attempt to categorise the person because categorisation is a normal part of our everyday cognition. For example, you may enter a lift (elevator) in an expensive hotel and find yourself standing alongside a man dressed in a business suit. Without necessarily being fully cognizant of it, you take note of his attire and the context in which he is situated and you are fully comfortable with the fact that he fits in the context and therefore presents no cause for concern or further deliberation. If, on the other hand, you find that the man is dressed in dirty fraying clothes, looks unwashed and smelly, and is carrying a bulky bag with him, you may note that his appearance does not fit with what you would usually associate with the context of an expensive hotel and you may wonder what his story is, whether he is lost, whether he needs help, etc. The point is, we categorise continually and most of the time subconsciously, in order to navigate our environment.

The process of putting people into categories has implications for communication in general and intercultural communication in particular. MacRae and Bodenhausen (2000) further explain the cognitive process of categorisation:

> Given basic cognitive limitations and a challenging stimulus world, perceivers need some way to simplify and structure the person perception process. This they achieve through the activation and implementation of categorical thinking . . . Rather than considering individuals in terms of their unique constellations of attributes and proclivities, perceivers prefer instead to construe them on the basis of the social categories (e.g. race, gender, age) to which they belong, categories for which a wealth of related material is believed to reside in long-term memory. Of course, it is also through the activation of categorical thinking that perceivers are sensitized to the presence of unexpected information. After all, one can only be surprised by a person's behaviour if one has prior expectations about how that individual should behave (p. 95).

Our motivation for wishing to place people in categories may lie in our aversion to uncertainty. One of the well known theories in communication is Berger's (1979; 1986) *Uncertainty Reduction Theory* (also Berger & Calabrese, 1975). The basic premise of this theory is that humans are uncomfortable with uncertainty and therefore the primary motivation behind communication in initial interactions is to reduce uncertainty. Two types of uncertainty are identified, namely, cognitive and behavioural. Cognitive uncertainty has to do with uncertainty about a person's attitude and beliefs that influence his or her thought processes. Behavioural uncertainty refers to one's inability to predict how the other person will behave in a given situation. Though the Uncertainty Reduction theory is not intended to specifically address intercultural situations, cognitive and behavioural uncertainty are arguably higher in intercultural spaces. Having been enculturated to into a particular worldview, one is presumably familiar with the values and beliefs that influence the thinking and behaviour of the people in that culture. When the situation involves a person of a different culture, however, the level of uncertainty is likely to be much higher. Uncertainty Reduction theory provides an explanation for why people ask questions to gather information, in initial interactions (such as, "What do you do for a living?" and "Where are you from?").

Considering the process of categorisation in light of Uncertainty Reduction theory, it is fair to say that this information gathering process in initial interactions also helps us to determine the correct category in which to place a person so that we know how to relate to him or her. We determine whether we have something in common with that person, whether we are familiar with the same topics with which that person might also be familiar, and perhaps even whether we like or dislike that person (based on the category in which we place the person).

In the process of categorisation, we may use a myriad of variables which we perceive to be relevant. These variables may range from occupation, gender, nationality, etc., to height, weight, and skin colour. What each of us considers as a relevant piece of information, of course, varies. Regardless, we first place people in categories and then decide how we would interact with them.

Categories are fluid. A person might shift from one category to another in someone's mind, based on further information gathered as interactions with that person proceed. For example, you may categorise a man whom you meet at a party as arrogant, based on the fact that you overheard him speaking extensively about a book he had recently published. Upon getting another chance to interact with him during the course of the evening, you may discover that in general he is an amiable and pleasant person, quite contrary to the qualities that belong to the category of "arrogant" in your schematic framework. Hence you may re-categorise the man as "pleasant" instead. But this process of re-categorisation (based on further information) may not happen if, at the initial stage of categorisation, you decide that the man belongs to an unfavourable category and hence proceed to terminate any further interaction with him.

Imagine the consequences of the process of categorisation in situations where elements of ethnicity and race are involved. For example, if people are in the habit of putting others who sport a certain skin-tone into a category to which they assign a derogatory meaning, then they are likely to cease further interaction with anyone who belongs to that category, merely based on first glance. This brings any possibility of dialogue or room for friendship to a screeching halt. The simplistic act of putting large groups of people into generalised categories based on physical attributes or other superficial criteria is one form of stereotyping.

One of the most important distinctions we make when we meet a person for the first time is to identify whether s/he belongs to our ingroup or not. As Gudykunst and Kim (2003) explain, "our ingroups are groups with which we identify that are important to us and for which we will make sacrifices" (p. 13). There are multiple ingroups with which we may affiliate based on different criteria, such as our religion, nationality, family, profession, etc. Research shows that we are predisposed to evaluating those whom we perceive as part of our ingroup in a favourable light. We also expect members of our ingroup to hold similar values to ourselves. Kim (2008) explains:

> . . . individuals identify with a group in a manner that is self-serving. The way people experience cultural identity is essentially not a rational but an emotionally driven experience. When it comes to our relationship to an outgroup in competition or conflict, we are less than likely to be fair and objective, and more likely to be irrational and defensive, favouring our ingroup and discriminating against the outgroup that threatens our ingroup (p. 361).

Considering the fact that our group distinctions are based on symbolic (and often arbitrary) differences, it is sobering to recognise that the perception of someone as an outgroup member can instigate animosity and even violence, given a mere shift of cognitive boundaries can instantly make them a member of our ingroup.

Ingroups and outgroups are fluid structures. Two people who consider the other as a member of the outgroup based on one criterion may find that they are both members of the ingroup based on a different criterion. For example, a Canadian engineer and an Australian engineer may consider the other person as a member of the outgroup when nationality is the salient variable. If profession were to become the salient variable, then they would both belong to the same ingroup. The year 2009 saw what is proclaimed to be the end of over two decades of civil war in Sri Lanka. The conflict was between two ethnic groups, the Tamils and the Sinhalese. Though to an outside observer these two groups of people may appear quite similar in physical appearance, to the Sri Lankan people the difference in language and ethnic heritage between these two groups of people were significant enough to classify the other as a member of the outgroup. On the one hand, the boundaries are drawn between the Buddhist Sinhalese and the Hindu Tamils, while on the other hand Sinhalese and Tamil people who share Christianity as the common religion see one another as members of the ingroup when religion is the salient variable.

Ingroup—outgroup distinctions bear great significance to intercultural communication. Not the least of which is the matter of attributing behavioural generalisations to a group of people, otherwise known as stereotyping. In fact, the process of categorisation that is so vital to our day-to-day functioning is also at the root of stereotyping.

Stereotypes

Stereotypes are cognitive structures that represent behavioural or character generalisations about a group of people. For example, "All athletes are arrogant" is a stereotype, but "My neighbour who is an athlete is an arrogant man" is not. The former is a generalisation about a group of people (in this case athletes) while the latter is an observation about an individual. Stereotypes help us to navigate our infinitely complex world by providing us with manageable categories. In other words, if we are to know the characteristics and preferences of each individual we ever encounter, our mind is likely to become overwhelmed with all that information. By relying on stereotypes, we access general information about the group of people to which an individual belongs and use this information to relate to the individual. For example, if you meet a Buddhist man for the first time, you may not know how to relate to him straight away. But, reaching for your general stereotypical knowledge of Eastern religions, you may begin by asking something like, "Are you a vegetarian?" This assumption might not be accurate; however, the stereotypical information to which you have access provides a starting point to the conversation.

Historic events contribute to particular stereotypes that are collectively shared by people in a culture. Stereotypes are also often reinforced through literature and art (Saro, 2008). Most of us are familiar with several common stereotypes associated with national, racial or gender groups. We often use stereotypes to not only explain someone's behaviour, but also to predict it. For example, we may say something like, "Is he German? I bet he drinks a lot of beer!" That is a prediction of someone's behaviour based on a stereotypical understanding of the nationality to which he belongs. In actual fact, the person in question might not like beer at all. Or we may reason that an Indian colleague at work likes spicy food because she is Indian, using our stereotypical understanding of the category "Indian" as an explanation for the reason why this particular person likes spicy food. Obviously this logic would not work if the colleague who enjoys spicy food happens to be Norwegian. Nevertheless, we regularly use stereotypical information to explain and predict the behaviour of others.

Though the word "stereotype" has come to bear a negative connotation in most instances, stereotyping is not an inherently negative process. It is, in fact, a necessary part of social cognition. Going back to the discussion on categorisation, we categorise in order to be able to assimilate and process information efficiently in a world of infinite variations. When it comes to people categories, we associate behaviours with these categories and therefore engage in the process of stereotyping. For the most part, stereotypes merely provide a basis from which to interact with a person; a means of overcoming potential ambiguity. As long as you are flexible in allowing for variations within a category and have the ability to form new categories when someone does not fit into an existing one, stereotyping does not debilitate the communication process.

If, on the other hand, you are overly reliant on stereotypes and are incapable or unwilling to allow for variations within your categories, then stereotyping can hinder effective communication.

People who possess greater levels of *cognitive complexity*, the ability to form many unique categories in one's mind, rely less on stereotypes compared to others (O'Keefe & Sypher, 1981). This is because cognitive complexity allows a person to recognise and register finer distinctions in other people, thus diminishing the need to rely on broad generalisations. For example, a new migrant to the United States might initially have a single category in which he puts "Americans." As time goes by, however, he might begin to notice certain regional differences in American people, and perhaps differences based on social class, education, travel, political views, and spiritual beliefs. If he is a cognitively complex person, he will begin to form new categories in his mind based on the new information he continues to acquire, to the extent that after a while, his framework of "Americans" is no longer one amorphous group, but instead several unique categories with rich details and variations. Gudykunst and Kim (2003) explain that a person's cognitive complexity in a given area is not static, but develops over time with different experiences. Contrary to cognitively simple people who are inclined to only pay attention to information that is consistent with their existing beliefs, cognitively complex people notice unique and new things. Hence cognitive complexity facilitates the deconstruction of stereotypes.

Given stereotypes are necessary for regular socio-cognitive processes, it isn't possible to eliminate them. It is, however, possible to change them. There are three models of stereotype-change identified in literature (Weber & Crocker, 1983), namely the bookkeeping model, conversion model, and subtyping model. According to the *bookkeeping model*, stereotype change occurs when a person encounters a number of instances which contradict an existing stereotype. As these incidents accumulate, there comes a point of saturation at which the stereotype is deconstructed. In order for this process to work the person needs to take note of each incident which contradicts the stereotype thus allowing for the accumulation of evidence. For example, you might have a stereotypical belief that police officers are rude. Then you encounter a situation in which your car breaks down and a police officer stops to help you. This incident contradicts your stereotype that police officers are rude. You take note of it. At another point in time you come across a police officer while hiking and enjoy a pleasant conversation with her. This too contradicts your prior stereotype. According to the bookkeeping model, as experiences like this begin to accumulate, you eventually reach a point at which you realise that your stereotype that all police officers are rude no longer applies.

Contrary to the bookkeeping model, the *conversion model* portrays stereotype change as dramatic onetime transformation which occurs as a result of an encounter with a significant stimulus which disconfirms an existing stereotype. Going back to the example of the stereotype that police officers are rude, perhaps you encounter a situation in which a police officer dives in front of you to save your life from a stray bullet in a drive-by shooting. According to the conversion model, such a dramatic experience might change your negative stereotype of police officers.

The third model describes a *subtyping* process where each significant disconfirming stimulus contributes to a process of differentiation whereby specificities are added to a large generalised group, thus breaking down the stereotype. For example, consider the stereotype, "Women are verbose." Perhaps you encounter women who are succinct, and notice that these women are from urban areas. So, you alter or you make a modification to your stereotype using the urban-rural subtype and conclude, "Women from rural areas are verbose." Then you encounter women from rural areas who are succinct and notice that these women are from small families. Then you make another modification based on the family size, and surmise, "Women from large families in rural areas are verbose." The process continues until the existing cognitive structures deviate significantly from the original stereotype, and the generalisation becomes increasingly specific.

As these three models reveal, stereotype-change is contingent upon a person being attentive to information that disconfirms an existing stereotype. There are ideal conditions under which a person is likely to take note of such information. A person who is under high load (high stress, high level of mental distraction) and low capacity (low cognitive complexity) conditions is unlikely to notice new information that disconfirms a stereotype. To illustrate this further let's revisit the example of the police officer who stops to help you when your car breaks down. Assume the breakdown happens in the middle of a highly stressful week at work, on your way to a crucial meeting for which you are already late. Your car screeches to a stop without warning and chaos ensues as other drivers start honking and trying to drive around you. You lift the hood and try to poke around to see what's happening. Some pedestrians wander over and take a look as well, offering you random pieces of advice. All the while your mind is frantic, thinking you are very late. It is under these conditions that the police officer walks over, tweaks a few things, and the engine starts running again. At the height of your stress and anxiety, you may not have the mental space to pay attention to the fact that the person who stops to help you happens to be acting in a manner that contradicts your stereotype of the group to which he belongs. You may be momentarily grateful, but the high load on your mind is likely to debilitate your ability to take note of and retain this key piece of information.

On the other hand, low load, high capacity, and high motivation to change stereotypes are ideal conditions under which one would notice an incident which disconfirms a stereotype. Returning to the example of the police officer once more, if your car happened to break down at a time when you were going for a relaxed Sunday afternoon drive, you may have the mental space to observe that it is a police officer, one whom you would have expected to act in a rude manner (based on your stereotype), who lends you a hand in an act of kindness that contradicts your stereotype.

But the ability to take note of information that disconfirms a stereotype alone is not sufficient. Motivation to change stereotypes is a key factor in deconstructing stereotypes. No matter how much disconfirming evidence is presented, if a person is unwilling to change a particular stereotype about a group of people, then the evidence is likely to be ineffective. Historical events show that certain stereotypes served the purposes of certain groups of people such that maintaining those stereotypes was vital to ensuring their way of life. For example, slave owners once justified their ownership of slaves by vehemently adhering to their stereotypical belief that dark-skinned people were ontologically inferior to light-skinned people. In such a situation, presenting logical arguments to contradict this belief would have been futile, because the stereotype not only served a functional purpose but also had dire moral implications, if proved false. Hence there are conditions under which even the presence of information that contradicts a stereotype does not lead to stereotype change.

 Negative stereotypes, when coupled with negative emotions about a group of people, represent racism, sexism, ageism, and the like. When prejudicial attitudes lead to prejudiced behaviour, it is called discrimination.

As discussed before, the process that leads to an act of discrimination is a complex one that cannot be simply chalked up to malice or evil intent. It starts with an everyday and necessary cognitive function of perception, followed by interpretation and categorisation. The way we categorise, as mentioned before, is influenced by our history, reinforced by our culture, and even rewarded by the people with whom we associate. Therefore a person could engage in an act of discrimination without malice, genuinely believing that his/her actions are justified. For example, having been saturated with cultural images that support male leadership and being in the company of those who are of the opinion that positions of leadership should be held by men, a person might choose a male leader over an equally qualified female one. However, by engaging in this course of action, this person further contributes to the existing social norms. Unless a person is motivated to change and has conditions and abilities that are conducive for stereotype change, changing the stereotypical mindset of a group of people can be challenging or even impossible. Given this, it is naïve to assume that merely providing information that disconfirms an existing stereotype can create positive results in the way of stereotype change.

There are significant reasons why a person or a group of people is resistant to changing existing stereotypes. Negative stereotypes concerning outgroup members, for example, can reinforce the values of the ingroup and perhaps even justify centuries of animosity between groups. If one were to suddenly recognise that the other group isn't as despicable as portrayed by the stereotypes, then the responsibility and regret of years of hostility and perhaps even acts of violence against the other group would be overwhelming. Hence, in such cases, it might be easier to adhere to the stereotypes than face the alternative. Often we dehumanise a group of people in order to justify hostile actions against them by harbouring stereotypes such as, "they are like barbarians" or "they are callous zealots." Having categorised a group as such, it may be easier to come to terms with acts of violence against them because they become dehumanised. But if somehow it were to be recognised that this group of people in fact consists of people just like us who hold the same hopes and dreams as people in our ingroup, then the social responsibility of actions against them and even the political ramifications of this recognition could be so monumental that it might be easier, at least at the subconscious level, to resist the stereotype change.

Cognitive Dissonance Theory

A possible explanation for why people are resistant to changing attitudes of prejudice is presented by the *Cognitive Dissonance Theory* (Festinger, 1957). The basic premise of the theory is that humans prefer consonance (equilibrium, balance) in their cognitions and, whenever inconsistency or dissonance in cognitions arises, we are in a state of discomfort and take measures to reduce this discomfort by bringing about consonance. *Consonance* exists when cognitions are consistent, such as "I want to lose weight" and "I am exercising." *Dissonance* arises when there is imbalance in cognitions, such as, "I want to lose weight" and "I am eating ice-cream." The magnitude of the dissonance is determined by the extent to which the issue at hand is significant to us. According to cognitive dissonance theory, when dissonance occurs we employ certain measures to bring about consonance. These are as follows:

Selective Exposure

In this method we seek information that supports our cognition. For example, consider the dissonance between the cognitions, "My country values equality for all people" and "There are hardly any minority persons in positions of power." To reduce the dissonance between these cognitions, one might seek information about how minority people are given equal opportunities as members of the majority, spend time with people who reinforce the belief that minority people are not in positions of power only because they choose not to be, and perhaps even look for evidence that members of the minority are better off not being in positions of power because of the resentment and discrimination they may face by holding such positions.

Selective Attention

When exposed to information that would create or increase dissonance, we engage in selective attention. We pay attention to everyday information that confirms our beliefs and tune out any information that might cause dissonance. This process sheds light on why some people vehemently hold on to what may clearly appear to others as ignorant and racist beliefs despite overwhelming evidence that contradict their beliefs. For example, some people may view immigrants as people who come to infringe on the jobs and privileges of the members of the host country. However, history reveals that many countries that attract large numbers of immigrants today such as Australia and the United States are in fact populated by a majority group that is not indigenous to the land. Hence the person who is considered a new immigrant is in fact merely new at a certain point in history. Members of the majority group in a country of immigrants could employ selective attention to justify an attitude of resentment toward new immigrants based on the reasoning that they have some prior claim to the country. However, this view takes into account a selective perspective of history which prevents them from acknowledging that they themselves were once immigrants to the land occupied by indigenous people.

Selective Interpretation

As its name indicates, selective interpretation is a process whereby dissonance is reduced or avoided by interpreting ambiguous information in a way that confirms existing cognitions. For example, a person who is prejudiced against a particular group of people might watch a movie in which two characters that belong to that group are portrayed; one lives a life of integrity and honour, and one lives a life that exemplifies every derogatory stereotype associated with that group. The prejudiced person watching the movie might interpret the movie to mean that despite the odd exception, the majority of the people who belong to that group live in a way that justifies the stereotypes.

Selective Retention

This method refers to our propensity for having a better memory for information that confirms existing cognitions, thus maintaining consonance. For example, consider a man who strongly dislikes people from a certain country because he believes they are loud and rude. Suppose he meets a shopkeeper from that country who is polite and courteous. This information is inconsistent with his existing cognition, and would cause dissonance. Suppose he comes across a few other members of that country and overhears them having a loud argument in the parking lot. At once his pre-existing cognition is supported, and he has better retention for this piece of information compared to the information that the shopkeeper, who was also from that particular country, was neither loud nor rude.

The tenants of cognitive dissonance theory help us to understand why people can be resistant to changing views that may appear to be irrational and even outrageous to others who do not subscribe to them. On an optimistic note, however, the quest for consonance can also take a more positive direction if stereotype change occurs in a person who was formally prejudiced against a group of people, then that person may use selective exposure to avoid friends who have prejudicial attitudes or dispose of books or music that promote previously held prejudicial views in order to maintain consonance between the newly formed cognitions.

While stereotypes represent behavioural generalisations about a group of people, inferences about individual instances of behaviour are explained in the process of attribution. Understanding attribution is an essential part of understanding intercultural communication because we often evaluate someone favourably or unfavourably without necessarily being cognizant of the reasons for our decisions. The level of ambiguity surrounding the reasons for the other person's behaviour is arguably higher in intercultural interactions. Therefore understanding the process of attribution is helpful in recognising instances when we may be inclined to make an unreasonable unfavourable evaluation of a person.

Attribution

Attribution is the process whereby we assign a reason for a particular behaviour. When we make an *internal* attribution, the behaviour is seen as arising from a personality trait. For example, if we see someone laughing hysterically and we conclude, "That person is crazy," that is an internal attribution. If on the other hand we make a situational inference for the behaviour and say, "He must have heard something very funny," then we make an *external* attribution, thus attributing the behaviour to the circumstance rather than a personality trait. Ross (1977) explains the notion of attribution theory:

> Attribution theory, in its broadest sense, is concerned with the attempts of ordinary people to understand the causes and implications of the events they witness. It deals with the "naïve psychology" of the "man on the street" as he interprets his own behaviour and the actions of others. . . For man, in the perspective of attribution theory, is an intuitive psychologist who seeks to explain behaviour and to draw inferences about actors and their environments (p. 174).

There are many factors that contribute to the decision of an internal or external attribution (Kelley, 1973). Consider the example of a woman crying in a restaurant. Suppose you know this particular woman and know her to be the kind of person who likes to do dramatic things to attract attention. Given this, there is *consistency* in her behaviour in that she usually does things like this to cause a scene. This would lead you to make an internal attribution. You also look for *distinctiveness*, by processing whether this person behaves like this in a variety of situations; and, knowing her flair for the dramatic, you once more make an internal attribution. Another factor you consider is *controllability*, evaluating whether it was within this person's ability to control this behaviour—if you conclude in the affirmative, then an internal attribution is once again the likely choice. Suppose this behaviour happens in a different context. Suppose you see this woman crying at a funeral. The *consensus* is that everyone arguably acts this way in a funeral. Hence an external attribution is made, reasoning that the cause of her behaviour was something circumstantial, not something to do with her personality. Thus there are four key questions that pertain to the process of attribution. First, you ask, "Does this person usually act this way?" If the answer is yes, then you make an internal attribution (*consistency*). Second, you ask, "Does this person act this way in a variety of situations?" If the answer is yes, this too leads to an internal attribution (*distinctiveness*). Third, you ask, "Did this person have control over this situation/behaviour?" If the answer is yes, once more the result is an internal attribution (*controllability*). Fourth, you ask, "Does everyone else behave this way in such a situation?" If the answer is yes, an external attribution is made (*consensus*). These questions neither occur in this order nor arise in every instance where an attribution is made. They do, however, provide us with a framework with which to understand the process of attribution.

To summarise, an internal attribution is where you assume that the reason for someone's behaviour lies within that person's personality. An external attribution is where you reason that someone's behaviour was caused by a particular circumstance. Consider another example; suppose you see a stranger yelling at a shopkeeper. If you conclude that the stranger is behaving this way because she is a ruder person, then you make an internal attribution. If, on the other hand, you conclude that the shopkeeper must have said something upsetting or that the stranger's behaviour must be the result of a very bad day, then you make an external attribution.

The process of attribution can be complex in intercultural contexts. We make behavioural inferences about other people based on our own understanding of the situation. Taking cultural differences into account, our understanding of the situation might not be as accurate as we believe. To consider a simplistic example, the behaviour of belching loudly after a meal is considered a compliment to the hostess in some Chinese cultures. For those who neither share in nor are aware of this value, this behaviour would appear crass and rude. In this situation, based on controllability and consensus (using one's own cultural frameworks), an internal attribution could be made erroneously, with the assumption that the person who belched at the table was behaving rudely. If the person making the attribution was aware of the particular cultural practices, however, she would have known that there is consensus in that cultural context and therefore she should have made an external attribution.

Let's view another example of a man (we can call him Adam) who is raised in a collectivistic and high power distance culture (for more information on high power distance cultures, and collectivism see Chapter 3). As such, it is ingrained in him from a very young age that he should respect his elders and authority figures and comply with their wishes, even if at times he may not agree with their point of view. Adam's friend, Brett, is from an egalitarian low power distance individualistic culture and has been raised to make his own decisions and follow his own path regardless of how the opinions of others. Suppose Adam's uncle informs him that he is going to be in town for a couple of weeks and that he would like to stay at Adam's apartment, despite knowing that Adam lived in a tiny studio apartment and having an extra person there for two weeks would be an inconvenience. Adam agrees, but complains to Brett about the difficult situation in which he has been placed. Brett is perplexed. He suggests that Adam should be frank with his uncle and inform him that it is not convenient for Adam to accommodate him. But Adam simply replies that he has no choice but to comply with his uncle's wishes. If Brett does not truly understand the deep-seated values of power distance and collectivism that influence Adam's behaviour, Brett would mistakenly assume that Adam had controllability in this situation and would make an internal attribution that Adam is simply a coward or spineless man when in fact, based on the cultural values that define Adam, he arguably does not have controllability in this situation. Further, in Adam's cultural context there is indeed consensus because everyone in Adam's position would indeed consent to an uncle's request for accommodation based on values of honouring one's elders and exhibiting family loyalty.

One of the most common errors in attribution is called the *Fundamental Attribution Error*, which occurs when we make an internal attribution when it was in fact situational variables which caused the behaviour in question (Ross, 1977; Ross & Nisbett, 1991). In other words, when we make a Fundamental Attribution Error (FAE) we overestimate the influence of the personality factors in causing a particular behaviour and underestimate the situational variables that contribute to this behaviour. For example, consider a situation where you see a colleague in a mall, looking directly at you. You smile and wave. But your colleague simply does not acknowledge your greeting. You may conclude that he is being rude. But if you find out later that he is near sighted and could not have seen you from that distance, then you would realise that you have made a FAE.

Stereotypes can facilitate fundamental attribution errors. For example, suppose Mark (who is not Asian) subscribes to the stereotype that Asians are racist. Suppose Mark goes to a store where the clerk happens to be Asian, and a little deaf, and fails to notice Mark when Mark asks a question. Reverting to his stereotype, Mark assumes the Asian clerk is snubbing him and thereby makes an internal attribution that the clerk is racist, and storms out of the store, having further convinced himself of his pre-existing stereotype that Asians are racist. In this example, Mark commits a FAE because he makes an internal attribution when in fact he should have made an external attribution because the behaviour he observed was caused by circumstance (the clerk's deafness) rather than personality preference (racism, as Mark assumed).

Conversation Break with Chris and Anusha

Anusha: Hey, my friend works for Ticket Master and he gave me this ticket to the basketball game on Saturday. I thought you'd enjoy it better.

Chris: Why would you think that? (Rolling his eyes exaggeratedly) You women think all of us guys automatically enjoy watching sporting events!

Anusha: No, I didn't get you the ticket because I thought you'd enjoy watching sports. Your new brother-in-law's team is playing that day and you mentioned you'd like to see him play sometime.

Chris: Wow, that's really thoughtful of you, Anusha. And I just committed a fundamental attribution error—based on a stereotype, no less!

Anusha: You're sounding like a textbook again. What do you mean?

Chris: First I evaluated you based on the stereotypical belief that because you're a woman you would, like many women, assume that men in general enjoy sports. And then I attributed your action of giving me this basketball ticket to an internal attribute, specifically that you are presumptuous. But your action was in fact motivated by an external factor—my statement that I'd like to see my brother-in-law play.

Anusha: (Grinning slyly) So, you committed a fundamental attribution error by concluding, "Anusha gave me this ticket because she is presumptuous"?

Chris: Precisely! I made an internal attribution when I should've made an external one.

Anusha: What if you had attributed my behaviour to my kindness? Isn't that also an internal attribution? So would that be a FAE also?

Chris: Well, if your action was instigated by the fact that you are a kind person then it wouldn't be an attribution *error*, would it?

Anusha: OK, but what if I'm not a kind person at all and merely gave you the ticket because you just happened to be the first friend I came across today—and let's say you concluded that I gave you the ticket because I'm a kind person. Is that a FAE?

Chris: Yes, because by definition a FAE is where you make an internal attribution when you should've made an external one. So, me concluding, "Anusha gave me the ticket because she is a kind person when I should've concluded Anusha gave me the ticket because I happened to walk by" is still a FAE.

Anusha: So, an internal attribution is when you reason that a certain behaviour is caused by something in the person's personality or nature while an external attribution is when you reason that the person behaved in that way in response to some external stimulus or reason—is that right?

Chris: Right! Like I said, I thought you gave me the ticket because you are presumptuous—obviously making an internal attribution, while the actual reason for your behaviour was a response to my statement that I'd like to see my brother-in-law's game. And so a FAE was committed!

* * *

As mentioned before, the way we perceive our environment is influenced by our schemata. We have expectations of "right" and "wrong" ways of doing things, polite and rude behaviour, appropriate and inappropriate ways of dressing, and even acceptable and unacceptable communication partners (people with whom we choose to communicate). We are constantly processing information within the context of our cognitive structures and making inferences based on this process. A person's perception is also influenced greatly by past experiences (Wyer & Gruenfeld, 1995). Even though our experiences as humans are similar (in that we all experience failure, success, loss, and excitement, regardless of the specific manifestations of these experiences) the nature of events that perpetuate these experiences are often culturally defined. The same incident may be perceived differently in different cultural contexts because of the social expectations and values that are part of the individual who is a member of that particular culture. These differences in perception influence the communication process.

The Relevance of Social Cognition to Communication

Social realities are constructed through rhetoric. Once we label something, it takes on symbolic significance and becomes real in our social landscape. The way we use language to communicate therefore continuously contributes to the creation of the social reality in which we find ourselves. Communication is a dynamic process. Each participant in an interpersonal interaction brings a unique set of variables to the interaction. These variables include personality, past experiences, cultural preferences, worldview, and situational variables. Individuals also have varying levels of self-awareness in the interaction. Additionally, individuals vary in their ability to adapt their own behaviour and expectations to the interaction at hand. An interpersonal interaction is therefore subject to many levels of complexity.

For example, consider an interpersonal interaction between two friends, Jason and Steve. Let's assume that the interaction pertains to Steve asking Jason why Jason had not returned his phone calls. Looking at the interaction from Jason's perspective, let us unpack the variables pertaining to personality, past experiences, culture/worldview, and situations that may influence Jason's communication. Perhaps Jason is an introvert who often prefers to have alone-time to recuperate whenever he has had a busy week surrounded by people. Given this personality preference, the reason why Jason had not returned Steve's calls may have been merely because Jason was having one of those times of recuperation. Perhaps there is a past history between Jason and Steve, such that Steve, being an extrovert, often invites Jason to parties and activities which Jason frequently declines. Being from an individualistic culture, Jason might have the expectation that he should be able to choose how he spends his time, given he is an adult and in control of his goals and decisions. Finally, perhaps this interaction unfolds at an end of a long day when Jason is tired and is not ready to re-hash what he perceives as a recurring conversation between Steve and himself. Thus Jason's introverted tendencies (personality), Steve's pattern of inviting Jason to parties (past experience), Jason's expectation that as an adult he should be able to spend his time as he wishes (culture), and the fact that Jason was tired (situation), may all contribute to how Jason responds to Steve in this situation. Obviously, Steve too is influenced by all these variables, as he sees the situation from his own perspective.

Many individuals have good intentions of communicating with others in an effective and appropriate manner. However, because of variations in individual perception, one person's idea of appropriate behaviour is not necessarily another's. One of the most overt examples of this situation is when the participants involved are from different cultures with different norms of appropriate behaviour. For example, consider Sheila who is from a culture where the most appropriate behaviour in interpersonal communication is to let the other person initiate the conversation and to hold back one's own opinions until those are solicited. Sheila's friend Ann is from a culture where you show respect to others by being forthcoming and straightforward, and you treat the other person as an equal. Sheila and Ann both consider themselves effective communicators, and both have good intentions of being respectful of the other. In an interpersonal exchange between Ann and Sheila, Ann expresses her opinions without holding back because she wants to convey to Sheila that she values Sheila as an equal and that she feels free to discuss her thoughts with her friend. Sheila, being true to her culture's norms of appropriate behaviour, listens to Ann's opinions and waits for Ann to invite her to share her own opinions.

The invitation, however, does not come because Ann assumes that Sheila would feel free to be forthright with her just as she has been with Sheila. Since both Ann and Sheila have good intentions of communicating well with each other, a conversation about their communication preferences follows. Ann asks Sheila why she has not shared her opinion about the topic of discussion. Sheila explains that in her culture it is inappropriate to express one's opinion unless it is solicited and that she was just trying to show respect to Ann by waiting to be invited to share her opinion. "But Sheila," Ann replies, "We are friends! You don't have to be so formal with me. Besides, I think your opinions are very important and therefore you shouldn't be timid about sharing them. I understand that that is how it is done in your culture, but you shouldn't feel restricted when you are talking to me." By these very words, Ann implies that Sheila's cultural perspective is restrictive and that her own way of communicating is "normal." Even though Ann validates Sheila's opinions by saying that she considers Shelia's opinions to be important, Ann does not validate Sheila's cultural norms for the way these opinions should be shared.

Understanding how we process information and how our perception contributes to our communication is imperative because, as illustrated by the example of Ann and Sheila, despite best intentions we may still end up communicating ineffectively or offensively because of our lack of understanding of perceptual processes.

Our use of language also communicates our collective biases toward certain groups. There is a US documentary called *The Colour of Fear* (Lee, 1994), in which some of the non-white participants express the view that, by way of labelling people groups as "African American," or "Asian American," the culture implies that to be just "American" is to be white. Even indigenous Americans are not just Americans, but "Native Americans." The labelling system implies that what is normal (the non prefixed American) is white and any deviation from the norm is represented by a prefixed label. Similarly, we often use the words like "Western" and "non-Western" when discussing certain countries or cultural groups. By doing so, the West is put in a central position or the vantage point from which we see the rest of the world. Though we may not intend to marginalize minority groups or promote ethnocentric attitudes, our use of certain labels inadvertently contributes to the ongoing creation of social reality. If we wish to change the dynamics in this reality, a key component of this change lies in rhetoric.

As mentioned in the introduction, today we live in a world where globalisation has blurred cultural boundaries in some parts of the world and yet in others cultural distinctions are being adhered to more rigidly than before. The national and ethnic classifications by which we operate automatically create ingroups and outgroups. These distinctions are further reinforced by our rhetorical choices. It is prudent for a student of intercultural communication to be alert to these factors and be informed of the social cognitive processes that influence our behavioural choices such that this information can be strategically used to both understand ourselves as well as foster an environment of cohesive cultural heterogeneity.

Mini Case Study

Conversation between Tim and Clark, who are both (white) university students, just out from class:

Tim: Man, today's lecture was intense!

Clark: Yeah . . . I'm still wrapping my brain around it.

Tim: I've never thought that Asian people or Lebanese people have so much hatred toward white people! I mean, those people on the video . . . they kept saying, "White people are prejudiced!" and "White people look down on me!" But I don't see them that way, you know? I've got so many friends from all over—I never think of them in terms of their skin colour!

Clark: I know what you mean. I mean, they come over here, and then they complain! If I go to their country I'll be like, I'm the foreigner so I better just adjust, you know what I mean?

Tim: I guess it must be hard to live in a new country. But I don't think it's fair to judge all white people by the few bad ones they may have met. I mean, I think we have equal rights for everyone. If you're right for a job you can get it, every citizen is eligible for government benefits . . . so I think if you want to live in peace and get al.ong with everyone then you can.

Clark: That's just it! I think some of them come here already with prejudice and then blame everyone else for it. I mean, if you want to make friends with white people and integrate into the new culture, then why would you keep sticking to your own groups and cliques of Asian people or Lebanese people? That's just rude, if you ask me.

Tim: I've never lived anywhere else, so I don't know what it'd be like to be new in a place. I guess I may be tempted to stick to other people from my country or at least those who speak English. But still, I think I'll try to mix with locals. . . .

Clark: Of course you would! Like I said, it's just rude to be cliquey and then blame white people for being prejudiced! I mean, why would I want to go mingle in Chinatown? If I want to experience a different country I'll just go there! In my own country I'd like to be normal, thank you very much.

Tim: I think I'll talk to some of my non-white friends and ask them whether they feel discriminated in anyway. I never thought to ask that question because I assumed . . . I wonder if some of them feel the same way as those people on the video. . . .

Clark: I doubt it! I think they interviewed just the radicals to exaggerate the point and make things dramatic. You know how these documentary producers are . . . it's all about making a splash.

* * *

Conversation between Wei Tan and Farook, who also attended the same class as Tim and Clark:

Farook: That was pretty intense!

Wei Tan: Yeah, I could almost feel people staring at me every time the Asian guy in the video kept saying, "White people are racist!"

Farook: I know! It wasn't so bad when the Black guy was talking because I was like, hey, I'm not black! But when the Lebanese woman started saying all those things about prejudiced white people I know people were looking at me.

Wei Tan: I don't quite agree with everything that was said, though some points are true.

Farook: Sure, there are nice white people and then racist ones. Like there's this shop owner who refused to serve my brothers the other day, muttering he doesn't deal with foreign terrorists.

Wei Tan: What?!

Farook: Yeah, happens all the time. People get a little freaked by Muslims these days. But obviously that guy had a problem.

Wei Tan: How can you stand it? You were born and raised here, right? You're just as much a citizen as any other white person!

Farook: I guess. But I can't help it if I don't have the right "looks" to be a full-fledged citizen! [Shrugs and grins]

Wei Tan: I don't know how you're so calm about it. I haven't really experienced discrimination like that, but I take certain precautions. I don't deal with white people unless I really have to. They don't want me here, so why pretend I want to be friends with them? I don't hate them or anything—not at all. I just think it's best to live and let live. . . .

Farook: Maybe. But I really don't care where anybody is from. I just think it's best to just be friends with whoever you get al.ong with—no matter where they're from.

Wei Tan: That's a good philosophy in theory, but hard to practice. Even if you want to be friends with someone, what if they don't want to be friends with you? What if they look at you funny all the time and talk to you slowly and loudly like you're a moron?

Farook: [Shrugs again]. There are prejudiced people everywhere, I guess—no matter what nationality they are from. We can't judge everyone based on those few people.

Wei Tan: It must be nice to live in your fairyland, man!

Questions to Ponder

Think about the conversations between Tim & Clark and Wei Tan & Farook in light of what you have read in this chapter.
1) With which character do you agree most?
2) Which character comes across as a racist or prejudiced person and why?
3) Which character comes across as someone who has a realistic understanding of things and why?
4) Have you gained any new insights from discussing this case study?

Chapter Two
COMMUNICATION STYLES AND
SYMBOLIC COMMUNICATION

When I was a child my friends and I used to play a game called "coffeepot." The game goes something like this: you select someone to step out of the group; then collectively you decide on a verb that you'd like the other person to guess; then the person is invited back into the group. The person may then proceed to ask the group various questions for the purpose of discovering the verb, by substituting the word "coffeepot" wherever the word would appear in a sentence. For example, suppose the verb is "eat." The person might ask the group, "How often do you coffeepot?" And the group would respond, "mostly three to four times a day" or something to that effect. The person goes on to ask such questions until s/he figures out the verb selected by the group. Despite the fact that a word is substituted in place of a verb, the participants of the game are able to communicate effectively without any trouble—simply because everyone has agreed that, in the context of the game, a particular word ("coffeepot") would act as a place-keeper for a variety of verbs. This game brilliantly illustrates the symbolic nature of language.

We live in a symbolic social world of our collective construction. Imagine driving through traffic on a regular day. We know to stop when we see the red traffic light and to start driving again when the light turns green. We know what a traffic light is, for that matter. We read road signs and understand what they mean. We know not to turn into a one-way street by the direction of the arrow. These are all symbolic entities that provide structure and conceptual frameworks within which we navigate life. These symbolic entities communicate certain messages that we collectively understand—because we have collectively assigned the meaning for which each symbol stands.

In order to comprehensively engage the complexities of intercultural communication, it is necessary to first understand the symbolic nature of communication and the way in which we co-construct social realities through the use of symbolic codes. In this chapter, communication as a symbolic activity and the implications of cultural differences in assigning meaning to symbols are discussed.

Symbols and Construction of Social Reality

Communication, intercultural or otherwise, is a symbolic activity. As such we co-create and operate in a social reality that is constantly morphing and changing with time and events in history. A good place to begin the process of understanding symbolic communication is to look at the work of Mead (1934) and Blumer (1969). Based on these scholars' work, the basic premise of *Symbolic Interaction Theory* is that our behaviour in a given situation is influenced by the meaning we assign to the people and/or things involved in that situation. Further, SI theory proposes that meaning is neither inherent in a thing, nor a person, but it is instead created in social interactions. Meaning is created and conveyed symbolically through language.

According to SI theory, thinking, or "inner conversation," influences the way we interpret symbols. Even the concept of self, SI theory claims, is socially constructed. The theory expresses that humans are continually adjusting our own behaviour according to the actions of other people, and in order to do this, we first interpret or assign meaning to other people's actions. Social reality is created and negotiated in this process of interpretation.

This notion has significant implications to intercultural communication, because the co-creation of social meaning happens within the context of cultural groups, each group assigning certain variations of meaning to the same signifiers. Cognitive sociologist Zerubavel (1997) characterises a signifier as something which represents or "stands in" for something else. In other words, a *signifier* is the symbol that represents the *signified* (the meaning of the symbol). Zerubavel explains, "Convertible cars likewise may signify free-spiritedness, whereas cigars are often associated in our minds with virility" (p. 68). What a signifier signifies varies from culture to culture. For example, white coloured attire is seen as a sign of purity in some cultures (such as a bride wearing a white wedding dress) while in others it is a sign of mourning. Similarly, black attire is considered formal wear in some contexts and a symbol of mourning in others (such as a black cocktail dress versus a black funeral dress). As these simple examples illustrate, cultural and contextual differences in the designation of meaning to symbols can cause communication challenges because, as mentioned before, communication is inherently a symbolic activity.

Discussing the idea of symbolic communication further, Zerubavel (1997) distinguishes between symbols, icons, and indicators. According to Zerubavel, an *indicator* is a signifier which has a natural association with that which it signifies. For example, smoke may indicate the presence of fire. In this example, smoke is an indicator. A *symbol*, on the other hand, is a signifier which in no way resembles the signified. For example, the word CAT does not resemble (in its appearance) the animal cat in any way. Hence CAT is a symbol. Zerubavel further identifies another signifier that is conceptually in-between an indicator and a symbol—he calls such a signifier an *icon*. An icon, though not possessing a natural association with the signified, does bear some resemblance to that which it signifies. For example, a picture or drawing of a cat, though still a signifier of the animal cat, bears some resemblance to the animal compared to the word CAT. Consider another example to illustrate all three forms of signifiers, all of which communicate clearly even to the extent of eliciting a physical response from us. The signified in this example is a tasty meal. A picture or photographic representation of this tasty meal is an example of an icon; it could cause a person to salivate in anticipation of what it signifies. A written description (symbol) of this tasty meal could also have a similar effect. Further, the smell of this tasty meal (indicator) also elicits a response of anticipation.

Relating Zerubavel's distinctions to intercultural communication, it can be reasoned that indicators and icons are more easily translated across cultures than symbols. Ordering at a fast food restaurant in a country in which the menu is written in a different language is easier than ordering in a high-end restaurant, for example, because fast food restaurants tend to have photographic illustrations of their meals to which one only needs to point. In an upscale restaurant, on the other hand, meal descriptions (symbols) are not always accompanied by pictures (icons). Icons thus facilitate communication in situations where there is a language barrier. Similarly, indicators are also more accessible in cross cultural situations compared to symbols. In other words, it is easier to smell smoke and figure out that there must be a fire than to understand the words "there is a fire" spoken in a different language.

Popper's Three Worlds

To further understand the nature of social meaning, let us turn to philosophy for a moment. Popper and Eccles (1977) describe our ontological realm of operation in terms of three worlds: World 1 consists of physical artefacts occurring in the natural world, World 2 consists of the subjective human experiences within the mind, and World 3 represents the world of knowledge which consists of artefacts from World 2 that have been objectified through communication. For example, if someone thinks of an idea, that is a World 2 artefact. If she communicates this idea to another person, then it becomes a World 3 artefact. In other words, language enables us to communicate our subjective experiences to others. Language enables us to co-create social reality. Berger & Luckman (1966) explain:

> Language provides me with a ready-made possibility for the ongoing objectification of my unfolding experience. Put differently, language is pliantly

expansive so as to allow me to objectify a great variety of experiences coming my way in the course of my life. Language also typifies experiences, allowing me to subsume them under broad categories in terms of which they have meaning not only to myself but also to my fellowmen. As it typifies, it also anonymizes experiences, for the typified experience can, in principle, be duplicated by anyone falling into the category in question. For instance, I have a quarrel with my mother-in-law. This concrete and subjectively unique experience is typified linguistically under the category of "mother-in-law trouble." In this typification it makes sense to myself, to others, and presumably, to my mother-in-law (p. 39).

We understand what "mother-in-law trouble" entails, even if we have not experienced it subjectively, because we are privy to the socially constructed concept of "mother-in-law trouble." To carry this line of thinking further, consider the concept of rude and polite behaviour. Each culture has its own norms of etiquette to which its members are expected to adhere. What is considered polite behaviour, however, is agreed upon collectively and communicated and reinforced through language. For example, when a child behaves in what the parent perceives as a rude manner, the child is corrected by the words, "that's rude!" or "polite children don't behave that way." The child then goes on to become an adult with the knowledge of what is considered polite behaviour in the society in which he/she is raised, presumably passing on this knowledge to his/her own children.

Arguably, this information about norms of etiquette in a particular cultural context is not as accessible to someone who is not part of that context as it is to someone who was raised in it. Hence at the most basic level when we expect "common courtesies" from another person, we inadvertently expect that person to have some level of familiarity with what "common" entails in our cultural context. This expectation is not always reasonable in intercultural spaces. But unless we are cognizant of our assumptions of familiarity, it is inevitable that we would be frustrated or disgruntled with the culturally different *other* who is unable to decipher the subtle nuances of the social reality with which we are familiar.

To further understand the nature of the social construction of reality, consider the concept of citizenship. One's citizenship is a required form of identification for a variety of social functions ranging from international travel to application for school admission. If one were to simply choose not to be a citizen of any country, it would be nearly impossible for that person to function in society given the extent to which the concept of citizenship is woven into the legal system (which in turn is another socially constructed entity). We have reified the concept of citizenship such that it is no longer open for debate—it simply is. Berger and Luckman (1966) explain reification as,

the apprehension of human phenomena as if they were things, that is, in non-human or possibly supernatural terms. . . . . Reification implies that man is capable of forgetting his own authorship of the human world, and further, that the dialectic between man, the producer, and his products is lost to consciousness (p. 89).

Though citizenship moderates tangible matters such as population numbers in a given land space and the distribution of resources, the idea that a person gets to be a member of a group of people who ally themselves with a particular piece of land is a socially constructed one. If we were to dismantle the idea of citizenship today, there is no question that it will cause major social and economic ramifications that are almost unthinkable. But this in turn reveals the extent to which we have reified citizenship. John Lennon's famous song, *Imagine*, attempts to look past reified symbolic concepts as the lyrics attempt to persuade the listeners to imagine a world without social boundaries. If concepts such as citizenship and patriotism are socially constructed, and as such arguably open to negotiation, why then do we go to the extent of even literally laying down our lives to defend these symbolic entities? It is necessary to explore this question in order to understand the power of the symbolic system we have constructed for ourselves through communication.

A possible answer for the reason why we have created and maintained these powerful symbolic systems is presented in the *Terror Management Theory* (Greenberg, Pyszczynski, & Solomon, 1986; Solomon, Greenberg, & Pyszczynski, 1991a; Solomon, Greenberg, & Pyszczynski, 1991b). Two basic assumptions under gird the theory: first, humans are endowed with an instinct for survival, not unlike other animals; second, unlike other animals, humans have higher cognitive abilities which enable us to be aware of and contemplate our own mortality. According to the theorists, the tension between the instinct to preserve life and the inevitability of mortality creates an *existential terror* in humans that must be squelched. Using their higher cognitive abilities, humans therefore create a symbolic system with which they associate, a system that will outlive their own individual mortality. Thus, culture is created and cultural worldviews are formed. These cultural worldviews "imbue the world with meaning, order, stability, and permanence, and by so doing, buffer the anxiety that results from living in a terrifying and largely uncontrollable universe" (Solomon et al., 1991b, p. 96). Though this is not its sole function, culture serves as a means of achieving symbolic immortality. The theorists further explain that the existential terror is held in check by a *cultural anxiety buffer*, which consists of 1) faith in a cultural worldview and 2) the knowledge that one is living up to the expectations of that worldview.

The sobering extent to which the symbolic systems (which we ourselves have constructed) exert influence on us is apparent in empirical studies which reveal that in conditions where people are reminded of their mortality, they have heightened favourable reactions toward those who subscribe to their cultural worldviews, and heightened aversion to outgroup members and those who are perceived as a threat to their cultural worldview (Greenberg, et al., 1990; 1992; Rosenblatt, Greenberg, Solomon, Pyszczynski, & Lyon, 1989).

Building on the findings of the Terror Management theorists, Morgan et al. (2002) draw a direct connection between the strength of the cultural anxiety buffer and intercultural communication behaviour, in the *Threat Buffer Theory*. Morgan and colleagues explain:

> To confront another system of values in another culture is to glimpse a place where our own extended efforts at achieving some measure of worth can potentially amount to very little. In another culture, we can have almost no value, while in our own culture, we may be a highly valued member of society. Thus, recognising the validity of another person's culture is in some small way, to chip away at the survival of our own sense of self, however symbolic that survival may be.
> Of course, our informal observations tell us that some people are much better at adapting to the customs and communication practices of other cultures. We would argue that there are degrees to which one's threat buffer, comprised of faith in a cultural worldview (the meaning dimension) and a sense that one is meeting the standards of value specific to that worldview (the value dimension), is developed (pp. 8-9).

The theorists further claim that the *meaning* and *value* dimensions of the *threat buffer* are such that if one of the dimensions is weak, the other may compensate for it by being stronger. For example, the theorists suggest that those who are low in the value dimension due to lack of familial connections or spiritual beliefs may compensate for this by working hard on their professional life and achievements to boost their meaning dimension. The strength of the threat buffer, the theorists argue, itself is fluid, varying with circumstances such as personal achievement or external threat to one's cultural identity.

Though the Threat Buffer theory has not been sufficiently empirically validated, it too provides a framework with which to understand the extent to which our symbolically constructed structures of meaning influence our intercultural behaviour. The theory provides an explanation, for example, as to why some people may be vastly resistant to adapting to a new culture compared to others. If both your meaning (the extent to which a person feels as a useful contributor to society) and value (a person's sense of how well he/she is living up to the expectations of the culture or spiritual beliefs) dimensions are strong, then you are arguably better equipped to engage effectively with other cultural worldviews without feeling threatened.

Conversation Break with Chris and Anusha

Chris: Why do you look so gloomy?

Anusha: (sighs). I had this opportunity to interview for a potential job because the recruiters are going to be on campus tomorrow, but I can't do it because I don't have any formal clothes to wear to the interview.

Chris: What do you mean? I'm sure they're not expecting you to show up in an expensive suit or anything—after all we're just students.

Anusha: I know. But I took all my nice clothes to my parents' place over the weekend and I don't even have a casual dress or a pair of khaki pants—all I have are cut off jeans and a t-shirt!

Chris: So what, wear those.

Anusha: *What?* I can't wear cut off jeans and t-shirt to a job interview!

Chris: Why not?

Anusha: (Looking at Chris incredulously) because they'll think I'm a belligerent, irresponsible weirdo who doesn't know the first thing about being professional! It's not the impression I'm looking to make with a potential employer. . . .

Chris: That's interesting, isn't it? Of course I understand what you mean—and I agree. But it is interesting that we have collectively somehow agreed that a job interview cannot be experienced in cut off jeans and t-shirt without eliciting an unfavourable social response.

Anusha: Ah, you're talking about what we learned in class, aren't you? About reification?

Chris: Yep. Somehow we have reified this whole concept of formal attire such that we ourselves are bound by it even though it was an arbitrary concept to begin with. Now, if we deviate from it then there are social consequences! Ironic, isn't it?

* * *

Communication in intercultural spaces is not only influenced by preconceived expectations of familiarity with one's social norms but also by language. Even if two communicators are able to communicate in the same language in an intercultural space, the way in which each communicator uses and understands the symbolic entity that is language influences how the interaction unfolds. A simple illustration is available in the way in which English-speaking Americans, Australians, and British use English words in a variety of different ways.

The extent to which language plays a role in our perception of reality is addressed in the work of Edward Sapir and his student, Benjamin Whorf, in what has come to be known as the *Sapir-Whorf hypothesis*. In its extreme form, the hypothesis purports linguistic determinism, claiming that language shapes or determines our perception of reality. A softer take on Sapir-Whorf hypothesis is that language influences our reality (as opposed to determining it). Empirical evidence largely supports the latter version. Sapir (in Whorf, 1939) writes:

> It is quite an illusion to imagine that one adjusts to reality essentially without the use of language and that language is merely an incidental means of solving problems of communication or reflection. The fact of the matter is that the "real world" is to a large extent unconsciously built up on the language habits of the group. . . . We see and hear and otherwise experience very largely as we do because the language habits of our community predispose certain choices of interpretation (p. 134).

Sapir-Whorf hypothesis highlights the fact that language is reflective of cultural values, and, learning a culture's language is of great value in the process of understanding the ways of that group of people.

Understanding verbal language alone, however, is only part of the process of communication. Often an understanding of nonverbal cues as well as contextual references is necessary to communicate effectively. All of us have participated in implicit communication from time to time. You may recall, for example, saying to your good friend or spouse that goes something like, "I'll meet you after work at the usual place," knowing that your friend would not only know that the "usual place" is your favourite ice-cream parlour but also that you've had a particularly rough day at work that can only be smoothed by a stiff dark chocolate milk shake. This is because you have shared history with your friend, and, from experience she knows that you usually resort to heavy milkshake consumption when you are stressed and you prefer the dark chocolate shake at *Cream Shoppe* to the one at *Misty's*. When you have a shared history with someone, you can communicate implicitly, or in *high context* mode, as Hall (1976) calls it.

Though each of us has a unique style of communication, our style is influenced by our peers as well the cultural context in which we operate. Some of us prefer a linear style of communication where you are "to the point," precise, and concise, using communication in a functional way to accomplish specific goals. Others of us prefer a narrative style of communication where we speak in stories, describing rich details and painting a contextual picture for the listener. Some of us use each of these styles strategically, using the former for professional contexts and the latter for communication with friends or family.

Research shows that there are cultural preferences in communication styles. A good place to start the discussion on communication styles is to examine Hall's communication contexts.

Low and High Context Communication

According to Hall, some cultures gravitate toward a *low context style* of communication in which the meaning of a message is almost entirely contained in the verbal component of the message, with little room for ambiguity. Low context communication is verbally explicit and linear in style. Going back to the example of you inviting your friend to the ice-cream shop, had you communicated in low context mode you may have said, "I had a rough day at work. I need to unwind with a dark chocolate milkshake. Can we meet after work at the *Cream Shoppe?*" This message is linear in that it builds an argument as to why you need to meet your friend, and it is explicit because there is little ambiguity. Low context mode of communication is prevalent in Westernised cultures and highly industrialised cultures where there is great mobility of population and less opportunity, over time, to develop long collective histories. Low context mode of communication is also characteristic of individualistic cultures.

In contrast, *high context* mode of communication is implicit, often indirect, and the meaning of the message is largely contained in nonverbal and contextual cues while the verbal component is only part of the message. High context communication is subtle, and has great potential for ambiguity. As illustrated in the ice-cream invitation example, high context communication is endemic of situations where there is shared history between the communicators and the assumption that the other person is aware of the relevant cultural cues necessary to accurately decipher the message. High context mode of communication is often practiced in collectivistic cultures.

To a low context communicator, high context messages may seem vague and possibly frustrating. Beyond the mild interpersonal challenges, the lack of understanding of these different modes of communication can lead to serious consequences such as breaches in the justice system. Liberman (1990) explains how the Aboriginal people's high context mode of communication often causes misunderstanding and even miscarriage of justice in the central Australian judicial system. Because the Aboriginal culture values harmony, often a defendant simply agrees with whatever is asked of him so as to cause the least amount of conflict. Adding this predisposition to the high context mode of communication in which verbal language is not used as a rhetorical weapon (as is custom in a court of law), the Aboriginal person is left in a pliable situation where the authorities have the ability to enact a desired outcome, regardless of the status of the defendant's guilt. There is, however, no implied malice on the part of the authorities, in this example. It is included here to illustrate the point that the lack of understanding of cultural differences in communication styles can lead to sobering consequences.

This understanding is particularly crucial for those in positions of leadership. Often high context mode of communication is used in high power distant cultures where respect is communicated in both overt and subtle ways to those who are recognised as holding certain social status. Delicate matters are discussed implicitly, in order to avoid embarrassment for the other person, especially if the other person is of a higher status. Often communicators who are conversant in high context mode of communication use high context messages to save face for the other person. For example, in a case where a person in a position of leadership has given poor instructions, the subordinate might say something like, "I'm sorry, but sometimes I have trouble understanding instructions. That's probably why I made a mistake in filing these forms." A person who isn't attuned to the situation might mistakenly assume that the subordinate is admitting responsibility for the mistake. But in fact the subordinate is delicately saving face for the supervisor by stating, "Sometimes I have trouble understanding instructions." If this conversation was to unfold in a linear direct manner, the subordinate would've said, "I know I made a mistake in filing the forms, but the instructions were not clear."

The point to reiterate is that low context communicators value directness and therefore would prefer if someone directly refused a request, for example, instead of obliging out of obligation. What may be difficult to understand for someone who comes from an individualistic low context perspective, however, is that to those who are from collectivistic and high context (and often high power distant) cultures, refusing a request from a person of authority or causing someone else to lose face is not an option. Often leaders from low power distant cultures ask a favour of someone in their organisation, assuming that the person is at the liberty to decline the request if it is an inconvenience to him/her. But if the person is from a high power distant culture, declining a request from a person in authority is unacceptable. Therefore the person will do whatever it takes to oblige. To illustrate this point further, consider another example.

Meet Bill, a man from a Western culture in which individualism and direct, linear communication are valued. Bill is an owner of a small business which employs about thirty people from various countries. Given the company is fairly small, the employees interact closely with one another and with Bill in a friendly, comfortable environment. Bill sees himself more as a friend to his employees than their boss, and often socialises with his employees after work. One day Bill asks Ram, one the employees, whether he would come early the next day to help set up the room for a surprise farewell party for another employee. The conversation goes something like this:

Bill: Hey Ram. Would you mind coming early to help set up the chairs for Susan's farewell party tomorrow? I had arranged someone to do it but he cancelled at the last minute.

(Bill thinking: I know it's last minute but let me ask anyway, as Ram is usually willing to help. If he is unable to do it I'll ask someone else).

(Ram thinking: Tomorrow we have the committee meeting that I've to chair. I have so much work to do! But Bill knows that already, so he wouldn't have asked me to help unless he has no other options).

Ram: Er . . . Sure, if you need me to help I can. I'll make some adjustments to my schedule. . . .

Bill: Hey, I know you've got that meeting afterwards and if it's too much just say so.

Ram: No, no problem.

(Ram thinking: Of course I can't refuse a direct request from my boss. It is thoughtful of him to remember my meeting though. I'll just have to forgo some sleep tonight to finish my preparation).

Bill: Thanks, you're a champ!
(Bill thinking: Great guy. Always ready to jump in and help).

Ram operated under the (mistaken) assumption that Bill had considered the contextual cues (that Ram had a particularly busy day coming up with a lot of responsibilities on his plate) before asking him the favour, and assumed that Bill did so only because there was no other alternative. Ram also gave further cues by hesitating slightly before responding, and making a reference to his schedule. As Bill did not withdraw his request based on these cues, Ram agreed to oblige. Bill did give Ram a way out by saying that he could decline the request if Ram had too much to do. However, Ram, being a high context communicator, read the contextual cues (of Bill asking him for help despite Bill's knowledge of Ram's busy schedule) and read beyond the verbal content of the message, interpreting Bill's comment as just an exercise in politeness—which, from Bill's perspective as a low context communicator, was not, because he meant his words literally.

For his part, Bill operated under the assumption that, given he had never lorded over his employees or treated them as subordinates, Ram would feel free to decline his request for help if he could not oblige. Bill even explicitly gave Ram the opportunity to decline. Since the entirety of Ram's verbal exchange was affirmative, Bill assumed Ram was able to help without significant consequence. Both people had good intentions, but there was a breakdown of meaning because both parties assumed that the other was communicating in the same mode or style as him. Being the leader, had Bill been attuned to cultural subtleties, he would have realised that Ram had never declined a request from him in the past (thus Bill's observation that Ram was always willing to help) and made the connection to the fact that he, Bill, was an authority figure in Ram's life and therefore Ram would not be able to refuse any request made by him.

In the reverse situation, if the leader is the one who communicates in high context mode, then he (assuming the leader is male) needs to be aware that the others in the group may not be able to decipher the contextual cues given by him. He also needs to be sensitive to the fact that the others may not respond to his messages as hoped, because of their inability to understand beyond the explicit verbal content of the message, and that he may at times have to step out of his comfort zone and communicate in an explicit way. Similarly, as illustrated in the example of Bill and Ram, a leader who communicates in a low context mode needs to step out of his comfort zone and learn to decipher contextual cues. The responsibility for facilitating clear communication does fall on the leader, by virtue of his/her role as the leader or authority figure.

Though often an individual is inclined to use a particular style of communication for the most part, high context communication is conducive to communicating with persons with whom one has a close relationship. This is because in such situations there is shared history and experiences and therefore verbal explicitness is not as necessary as in a communication exchange between strangers or casual acquaintances. Low context mode of communication is functional when communicating with people with whom we do not share a history. Often people use low context communication in professional settings and high context messages in intimate familial or relational settings.

These dynamics operate in face-to-face communication. With the advent of new technologies, however, much of today's communication is done via e-mail, online forums, and other non-face-to-face media. McLuhan (1964) once said that the medium is the message; meaning the medium through which a message is communicated significantly and uniquely influences the meaning of the message itself. Face-to-face communication allows for the richest conveyance of nuances and various facets of meaning. Given high context communicators' reliance on nonverbal codes to convey much of the meaning, it isn't surprising that Rice, D'Amra and More (1998) found that communicators from cultures which use predominantly high context mode of communication preferred face to face communication compared to those from cultures where low context mode is prevalent. There is also some evidence to suggest that e-mail is perceived as a less formal medium than face to face communication, and as such, those operating in high context as well as high power distant cultures prefer face to face communication over e-mail (Richardson & Smith, 2007).

As mentioned earlier, from the perspective of a low context communicator, high context mode of communication might appear elusive, vague and perhaps even deceptive. This erroneous perception can exacerbate or even cause relational conflict. Similarly, a high context communicator might find the low context mode of communication to be abrasive, harsh, and lacking in tact. Cultural differences aside, it is necessary to recognise that individuals choose high or low context styles of communication either strategically to suit a relational context or by preference based on their personality or upbringing and therefore the recognition of both of these modes as valid means of communication may serve as the first step toward healthier communication exchanges.

To fully understand different styles of communication, it is helpful to understand how we use verbal and nonverbal codes. Verbal language has *denotative* meaning (the meaning formally assigned to a word; dictionary meaning, in other words) and *connotative* meaning (negotiated meaning which varies depending on context). For example, the word "sick" has the denotative meaning of illness or perhaps something vile, while it has a range of connotative meanings, including trendy, popular or something very good. When someone learns a new language, they mostly learn the denotative meaning of the words and are therefore at a disadvantage when it comes to conversing with the "locals" because we often rely on connotative meaning when communicating. In intercultural interactions it is helpful therefore to clarify the meaning of words from time to time, even if both parties speak the language fluently.

Verbal and Nonverbal Codes

There are several levels of translation involved when communicating in a different language (as is often the case in intercultural exchanges). As mentioned before, language competency alone does not always guarantee effective communication. At the most obvious level, translation happens at the *vocabulary* level where a relevant word needs to be chosen when speaking in another language. Additionally, *grammatical* translation is also involved, as sentence structures vary in languages such that, if one is thinking in one language and speaking in another, words have to be rearranged correctly before delivery. There is also the matter of *experiential* and *conceptual* translation that needs to be considered (Samovar & Porter, 2004). Idiomatic expressions aside (which also require translation), sometimes it is difficult to translate a certain concept from one language to another because not all concepts exist in all cultures. For example, the concept of sexual harassment may be familiar to certain cultures but not others. Further, certain experiential expressions may be difficult to translate. For example, a common expression used after a sumptuous American Thanksgiving meal is, "I'm stuffed," meaning I am beyond satiated and slightly uncomfortable due to the excessive amount of food I've consumed. For someone who has never in his/her life had enough food to fully satisfy his/her hunger, this expression would be not only hard to understand but also hard to translate.

Engaging in intercultural communication also involves the ability to navigate the use of various nonverbal codes. Though high context communicators rely more heavily on nonverbal cues to convey meaning, both high and low context communicators alike use nonverbal codes regularly. The purpose for which the codes are used, however, may differ in each case. It is helpful to identify the different types of nonverbal codes as well as the functions of nonverbal codes, to facilitate this discussion.

Nonverbal and verbal codes are similar in that they are both symbolic, patterned, and often idiosyncratic to cultural contexts. They are both used to communicate meaning, but when there is a contradiction between the verbal and nonverbal message we tend to believe the nonverbal. There are several types of nonverbal codes which can be identified, but a few of them are discussed here:

Kinesics

Originating from the research of anthropologist Ray Birdwhistell (1970), kinesics refers to the use of gestures, facial expressions, and body movement to convey meaning. Kinesics is often used in combination with other types of nonverbal codes but also can be specifically used to convey a particular meaning. For example, the extent to which one lowers the upper body when bowing shows different levels of respect in the Japanese culture. Kitao and Kitao (1988) argue that factors such as history, religion, familial relationships, etc. contribute to how people from particular cultural groups use kinesics.

The notion of emoticons in emails and online messaging technologies is based on the principles of kinesics (Ptaszynski et al., 2010). Even though there are cultural variations in the use of facial expressions, Eckman (1972) and several researchers since then have discovered that there are some facial expressions that are recognised and associated with the same emotions across cultures, namely happiness, sadness, surprise, fear, disgust, and anger.

Proxemics

The use of space and distance to convey nonverbal meaning is characterised by proxemics. The tradition of seating the honoured person at the head of the table or arranging the furniture in your office such that your chair is higher than that of the guests are examples of proxemics. One of the noticeable ways in which cultures differ in proxemics is in the use of personal space. On the one hand, people of some cultures are quite comfortable standing in close proximity to one another while conversing or queuing in shops. On the other hand, people prefer a personal "bubble" or space around them such that they become extremely uncomfortable if someone violates this space by stepping closer. Because of the diverse nature of today's society, I prefer not to categorise certain national groups as people who prefer more personal space as opposed to certain other national groups. In my experience I've found that preference for personal space varies from individual to individual, though there are some cultural predispositions based on upbringing. It is, however, useful to be aware of the concept of personal space because in some cultures it is an insult to stand further away from someone when conversing with them, while in others it is insulting to stand too close. Therefore two persons in an intercultural space could simultaneously insult each other by trying to be polite! Awareness of cultural differences in personal space can at least help the persons avoid making a fundamental attribution error (see Chapter 1).

Cultural preferences aside, personal space can also be violated strategically to intimidate or to convey affection. Burgoon's (1978) *Expectancy Violation Theory* provides a framework for understanding this process. The theory is based on the assumptions that our interactions with other humans come with certain pre-conceived expectations which are learned from previous experiences, and if these expectations are violated, then the result may be positive or negative depending on how favourably the communicator is perceived. When someone deliberately violates the expectation another person has of personal space, this gesture produces a physical and cognitive arousal in the other person. If the person at the receiving end perceives the "violator" favourably, then the violation heightens the initial favourable perception. But a deviation from expected behaviour can also result in heightened negative perception if there is little perceived reward value of the deviant. Burgoon's work is based on Hall's (1966) idea of proxemic zones (in which intimate distance, personal distance, social distance, and public distances are delineated), which resulted from observations of North American interactions.

Haptics

Haptics refers to the use of touch to convey meaning. Haptics can often be used when verbal language is inadequate or inappropriate. For example, when a friend is in deep grief, often a hug conveys comfort and solidarity much more effectively than words. There are cultural traditions that dictate haptics as well. Religious values often guide appropriate touching norms between men and women. People from some cultures are in general more socialised to show greetings and affection through touch than others. Such cultures are often referred to as "high contact" cultures as people in these cultures use haptics more demonstratively (Hall, 1966). Some researchers argue that high contact cultures are mostly located in warmer climates (Anderson et al., 2002). The proposed reasoning behind this is that people in cooler climates are task oriented due to the necessity of surviving harsh winters while people in warm climates are able to be relationship oriented. This may be an overly generalised way of conceiving cultural differences in haptics, but it provides one theory as to why these differences exist.

There are also cultural taboos concerning which hand one uses for touching. For example, some cultures consider the left hand as unclean as it is used to wash up after performing morning rituals. The inappropriate use of haptics can create challenges when communicating in intercultural spaces. A mindful communicator would carefully take note of haptic traditions in a cultural context and adopt the appropriate practices.

Vocalics

Also known as paralanguage, vocalics refers to the use of tone and volume of the voice in conveying meaning. In some cultures speaking loudly and exuberantly is normal practice while in others such volumes and tones are reserved for angry or excited conversations. In intercultural spaces, a "normal" tone by one person could be interpreted as disproportionally emotional by another, merely based on cultural differences in vocalics. Having lived in many countries, my own use of vocalics has been influenced by the various cultures with which I have come into contact. The extent of this influence was apparent when one time I overheard my father speaking in loud and passionate tones, and I rushed to ask my Mum, "Why is Dad upset?" To which she replied, "He's not. That's his normal way of speaking."

Vocalics can be used strategically to convey intimacy (whispering, for example), emphasis, power, intimidation, surprise, anger, excitement, and a variety of other meanings. It is important, however, to be aware of cultural differences in the use of vocalics, as mentioned before, in order to avoid misunderstanding the meaning of a particular vocalic code.

Chronemics

We not only use time to convey meaning, but also derive meaning from the way others use time. For example, if a person shows up fifteen minutes late for a job interview, the interviewer might infer that this person is either irresponsible or not very interested in the position. I recall one time when I had to wait for an hour and a half for a doctor's appointment, despite the fact that I had already made the appointment ahead of time. As I waited, it occurred to me that if that doctor had a son or daughter in university and wanted to see me about his child's studies then I could have been the one to make him wait! Chronemics conveyed who had the seat of power, in that situation.

We operate in formal and informal time, each with its unique set of rules. What constitutes formal and informal time also varies from culture to culture. The whole concept of time also varies from culture to culture. To illustrate this, I would like to share the following excerpt from Edward T. Hall's (1973) book, *The Silent Language*, which is considered one of the seminal pieces of literature in the inception of intercultural communication as a field of study:

> A requisite of our own temporal system is that the components must add up: Sixty seconds have to equal one minute, sixty minutes one hour. The American is perplexed by people who do not do this. The African specialist Henri Alexandre Junod, reporting on the Thonga, tells of a medicine man who had memorized a seventy-year chronology and could detail the events of the period he had memorized as an "era" which he computed at "four months and eight hundred years' duration." The usual reaction to this story and others like it is that the man

was primitive, like a child, and did not understand what he was saying, because how could seventy years possibly be the same as eight hundred? As students of culture we can no longer dismiss other conceptualisations of reality by saying that they are childlike. We must go deeper. In the case of the Thonga it seems that a "chronology" is one thing and an "era" something else quite different, and there is no relation between the two in operational terms (pp. 16-17).

In his later work Hall (2003) went on to make a distinction between what he calls *monochronic* and *polychronic* time. Hall characterises polychronic time as doing many things at once and monochronic time as doing one thing at a time. The distinctions in orientation to time have a behavioural dimension in how people structure their time and an experiential dimension in how people consider or feel about time (Todd, 2009). According to Hall, those who operate in polychronic time are orientated toward relationships and the completion of transactions as opposed to adhering to appointments or schedules (the latter being the preference of those who operate in monochronic time). Hall explains:

Matters in a polychronic culture seem in a constant state of flux. Nothing is solid or firm, particularly plans for the future; even important plans may be changed right up to the minute of execution. In contrast, people in the Western world find little in life exempt from the iron hand of M-time. Time is so thoroughly woven into the fabric of existence that we are hardly aware of the degree to which it determines and coordinates everything we do, including the moulding of relations with others in many subtle ways (p. 263).

Needless to say, when a person who operates in monochronic time interacts with a person who operates in polychronic time, there is great potential for frustration and misunderstanding. The person in M-time may assume that the person in P-time is being deliberately irresponsible or blasé while the person in P-time may consider the person in M-time to be uptight, rigid, and unreasonable.

Apart from the five types of nonverbal codes mentioned, there are other categories of nonverbal codes as well, such as the use of facial expressions and gaze. Eye-contact conveys great meaning regardless of cultural context. The specifics of how eye-contact is interpreted, however, vary from culture to culture. Just as prolonged eye-contact is considered disrespectful in some cultures, the lack of eye-contact is considered disrespectful and perhaps even devious in others.

Given the significant role nonverbal codes play in communication, it is prudent to understand cultural differences in the use of nonverbal messages. It is not hard to imagine how the differences in the way in which we use nonverbal codes can cause misunderstandings in communication that happens in intercultural spaces. People who participate in business ventures across cultures or work on team projects with people from a variety of cultural backgrounds are only too aware of how differences in perceptions of time, personal space, gestures, etc. add a measure of complexity (and often frustration) to the dynamics of the communication. Systematically understanding these differences facilitates communication in intercultural spaces.

We use verbal and nonverbal codes together in strategic and specific ways when we communicate (Knapp & Hall, 2007). Some of these ways include: 1) *Repeating*—When we say yes and nod at the same time, for example, the nonverbal code repeats the meaning of the verbal code in that the nonverbal alone without the verbal code would still have conveyed the intended message (in cultures where nodding is considered a sign of assent). 2) *Complementing*— Sometimes nonverbal codes are used to enhance or compliment the verbal message, such as smiling while you say, "I'm so happy!" Low context communicators arguably use nonverbal codes to repeat or compliment the verbal message more than to substitute for it. 3) *Substituting*—This is when nonverbal codes are used instead of verbal ones—such as frowning to show displeasure (or concentration, as the case may be). It is often advisable to avoid *substituting* when communicating in intercultural spaces if possible because, due to the differences in the use of nonverbal codes, there is a higher likelihood of the meaning being misunderstood 4) *Contradicting*—Sometimes nonverbal codes are used intentionally to contradict the verbal message, to convey a particular meaning. For example, one might playfully chide a friend saying, "You're a terrible person!" while grinning. Once more, contradicting can also be the cause of misunderstandings in intercultural spaces. Contradicting works most effectively in situations where the communicators are familiar with each other and the cultural context in which the interaction unfolds. 5) *Regulating*— Nonverbal codes can also be used to regulate the flow of conversation, such as using eye contact, raising one's hand to draw attention, leaning forward to indicate intention to interject, etc. I came across an interesting way of regulating conversation in a recent class in which I was a participant. Instead of using his voice to command the attention of the class, the professor simply raised his hand, and instructed the students that, in the future, whenever he raises his hand, the students must also raise their hands and simultaneously cease conversation— thus bringing the class to order in a quiet way.

Knowing the different kinds of nonverbal codes as well as the ways in which these can be used enables the communicator to be more cognizant and strategic in the use of nonverbal communication. This is particularly beneficial in intercultural spaces where there is great variation in the use of nonverbal codes and great potential for misunderstanding. In addition to understanding differences in the use of verbal and nonverbal codes, understanding different styles of communication is also beneficial. Even though many of us may intuitively recognise that some people use a different style of communication than our own, we may not be able to articulate what that difference entails or how to adapt our own style to match theirs if need be.

Mini Case Study

Kate and Jill are friends. They are also colleagues, with Kate being Jill's team leader. Jill is from a higher power distant cultural background while Kate is accustomed to a more egalitarian setting. Thus Kate behaves in such a way that her subordinates feel at ease with her and she enjoys friendship with many of her team members. A phone conversation between Kate and Jill unfolds as follows:

Kate: Hello Jill. I'm calling because I heard you're having a bridal shower for Jane on Saturday.

Jill: Err . . . yes, I am.

Kate: Hey, that's great. Can I come?

Jill: [Pause] Sure, of course

Kate: Really? That's great! Are you sure?

Jill: Yes, of course

Kate: I feel a bit badly that I sort of invited myself! Are you sure it's OK that I come? If it's not OK, please just say so. No hard feelings

Jill: No, of course you should come. I am sorry I didn't send you an invitation myself

Kate: That's OK. Thank you—I'm looking forward to it!

Questions to Ponder

1) What cultural elements or communication styles (if any) are at play in this conversation?
2) Contemplate the situation from each of Kate's and Jill's perspective
3) Contemplate the underlying implications illustrated by this exchange, in light of your knowledge of intercultural dynamics.

Chapter Three
CULTURAL DIMENSIONS AND CONFLICT NAVIGATION

"Culture" is often an over-used and under-delineated word. We use the word culture and variations of it in phrases such as "organisational culture," "popular culture," "cultural misunderstanding," "cultural event," etc. in everyday conversations. In each of these phrases the word culture is nuanced. Anthropologist Geertz (1973) views culture as something to be defined by those who are participants of it. He writes, "Societies, like lives, contain their own interpretations. One has only to learn how to gain access to them" (p. 453). Geertz's intention is to uncover the narratives of the locals of a culture, as a way of gaining access to their interpretation. Psychologist Bruner (1990) proposes that "culture and the quest for meaning within culture are the proper causes of human action" (p. 20). He goes on to say, "Given that psychology is so immersed in culture, it must be organised around those meaning-making and meaning-using processes that connect man to culture" (p. 12).

In today's society, mass media portals play a crucial role in shaping and reinforcing values and ideologies that we come to understand as "culture." Following in the footsteps of his predecessors of Marxist thinking, media researcher Gitlin (1972; 1980; 1982) paints the picture of a passive mass audience subject to manipulation by the media. Media, controlled by the bourgeois, is accused of reinforcing hegemonic practices that in turn control the proletariat. According to Gitlin, ideology, masquerading as entertainment, captivates the unsuspecting audience and influences its views – thus shaping culture. Gitlin's view is that through this process of reinforcing hegemonic practices, every society works to reproduce itself. Hegemonic practices of the bourgeois notwithstanding, the collective norms, values, practices, and beliefs that make up a culture morph over time, as witnessed by history, reflecting the migration patterns and significant historic events that impact a particular group. Though there are arguably infinite variations in cultural groups, it is helpful to understand the influence of culture on communication through a broader framework in which some commonalities can be generalised.

Dimensions of Culture

A few years ago I was appointed president of an organisation which consisted of about twelve board members, all of whom outranked me in age by at least a decade. To make matters worse, I knew relatively little about the organisation compared to most of them because I had not been with the group long. At the first board meeting which I convened as president, I could feel a tangible tension around the table. I had naively assumed that I would be warmly welcomed and mentored into my role, given the others were older and more experienced and given I had been asked to take that position of leadership at a time of crisis in the organisation. I thought the board members would see me as someone who was in need of their wisdom and guidance and as such would invest in my success. I was wrong. Instead of seeing me as a next generation leader whom they could mentor, they saw me as their competitor, a younger version to replace them and make them obsolete.

I recall contemplating the dynamics around the table that day. Given my Asian upbringing, I would have been more comfortable addressing the older men and women by their title and surname than by their first name. However, the Western cultural context in which I found myself at that time dictated that I address them by their first name, as my peers. But they were not my peers—not by far. And my attempt at adopting the social norm of informality was only contributing to a false sense of equality and fostering resentment. This is an example of a cultural dimension at play, namely power distance. In this chapter I will discuss some broad categories with which to understand cultural differences in communication and behaviour.

In one of the earliest attempts at gathering large-scale statistical data on cultural differences, Geert Hofstede (1980; 1984) surveyed IBM companies around the world and identified overarching cultural patterns or dimensions which influence people's behaviour in significant ways. To name four of the more well-known cultural dimensions, they are individualism-collectivism, masculinity-femininity, high-low power distance, and high-low uncertainty avoidance.

Individualism-Collectivism

Triandis (1995) identifies four attributes of this dimension: 1) individuals' perception of themselves 2) how individuals relate to other people 3) individuals' personal goals, and 4) the key concerns that drive individuals' behaviour. Individualism is characterised by a social mentality which focuses on the individual, valuing and recognising individual achievement, and encouraging independent thought and action. In contrast, collectivism is characterised by a communal mindset where the collective is valued above the individual, cooperation is encouraged (as opposed to competition), and expectation is placed upon individuals to behave in a manner that benefits the group even at the expense of individual goals. Sayings such as, "follow your dreams" and "pull yourself up by your bootstraps" are typical of an individualistic worldview while sayings such as, "one beam cannot support a house" and "two minds are better than one" demonstrate a collectivistic mindset.

A related concept to individualism-collectivism is the idea of group affiliation or ingroups and outgroups. Ingroups are groups of people with whom we feel an affiliation; those who do not belong to our ingroup are perceived as belonging to the outgroup. The concept of in and outgroups is fluid in that two Australians could be part of an ingroup at the Olympic games against other countries, but the same two persons can perceive each other as members of an outgroup when they are at home, supporting the Sydney Swans and the Brisbane Lions respectively. Gudykunst and Kim (2003) explain that while both individualists as well as collectivists belong to ingroups, the sphere of influence that an ingroup exerts on an individualist is less than that which it exerts on a collectivist. In other words, an individualist may belong to an ingroup of engineers who work for the same company—but that ingroup only influences the person's professional sphere. At home, she is not dictated by the values of that ingroup. A collectivist, on the other hand, sees the ingroup affiliations in a more holistic way and is influenced by the values of the ingroups to which he belongs even outside the specific realm of operation of a particular ingroup.

In a study to determine whether descriptive norms about one's cultural values and beliefs influence how a person makes attributions, Shteynberg, Gelfand, and Kim (2009) discovered that persons who had lower collectivistic values and beliefs ascribed more blame to a person if they perceived that that person acted intentionally. Further, they found that such individuals (lower in collectivistic values and beliefs) perceived that a violation of rights is more harmful than the violation of duty. Assuming individuals fall on a continuum of individualism to collectivism in their personal value orientation, these results reinforce the understanding that those with individualistic values and beliefs place higher priority on individual rights than individual duty. In the collectivistic mindset, however, individual duty would be of higher importance than individual rights. For a student of intercultural communication, this is a key point that must be grasped. The emphasis on individual rights is widely prevalent in media messages ranging from Hollywood movies to Westernised commercials. In such an environment it is not hard to dismiss someone who chooses duty over rights as weak-willed or archaic. However, in order to effectively communicate in intercultural spaces, one must recognise the presence of valid alternative perspectives based on deep-seated cultural values, even if one does not understand or agree with them.

Though Hofstede's research categorises countries as individualistic or collectivistic depending on a numeric score, recent research reveals that it is more meaningful to see individualism and collectivism as individual variables (that is, a person being more oriented to individualism or collectivism) rather than national variables (Cai & Fink, 2002). It is also possible that a person might have an individualistic perspective in professional settings and a collectivistic perspective when it comes to family matters. Generally speaking, however, it is helpful to understand the individualism-collectivism dimension as it explains certain cultural differences that cause communication challenges.

Masculinity-Femininity

Hofstede (1991) makes the distinction between masculine and feminine cultures by stating that masculine cultures are where gender roles are distinct such that men are expected to behave in stereotypically masculine ways and women in stereotypically feminine ways, while in feminine cultures there is overlap of gender expectations and roles. Hofstede also notes that cultures that are high in masculinity, value qualities that are stereotypically associated with masculinity such as ambition, assertiveness, achievement, etc., and cultures that are high in femininity, value nurturing, and greater relational quality of life. Gudykunst and Kim (2003) assert that those from masculine cultures tend to have limited interaction with members of the opposite sex compared to those from feminine cultures—a tendency that could cause communication challenges when people from these two types of cultures (especially if they are of the opposite sex) interact. It must be remembered that Hofstede's dimensions fall in a continuum, with each extreme being on either end and most cultures falling somewhere along the continuum.

Power Distance

In high power distance cultures, people are expected to value social hierarchy and employ behaviours such as using people's appropriate titles, deferring to those who are older, and using formality as a sign of respect. In cultures where power distance is low, despite structural hierarchy there are counter measures employed to create a sense of equality. For example, the CEO of the company might invite the employees to call her by her first name instead of her title and surname, as a way of creating rapport. It is not uncommon in low power distance cultures for students to call their professors by first name and the professors to expect students to challenge their points of view despite the fact that the professor has the intellectual seat of power in the classroom.

Going back to the example with which I opened this chapter, power distance (or lack thereof) can create subtle social tensions. On the one hand, in cultures where positions of power are overtly established and exercised, there is little room for ambiguity. There may, however, be room for resentment or feelings of oppression if those who are lower in the chain of power feel that they are not valued or taken seriously by those in the seats of power. On the other hand, as illustrated in the boardroom example, in lower power distance cultures a false sense of equality may be established through the practice of informality amongst those in the seat of power and those who aren't, but there could still be undercurrents of frustration and resentment because, the ones who are in positions of power remain so regardless of whether they are addressed by their first name or their title. That is, while the sense of egalitarianism in low power distance environments does facilitate open discussion, in actuality the manager has the power to fire the employee regardless of whether the employee calls him "Bob" or "Mr. Roberts." In this situation, there is no functional equality in power.

When discussing power, it is important to differentiate between different types of power. One of the most widely known pieces of literature on power is French and Raven's (1959) bases of power. Among these are legitimate power, expert power, coercive power, referent power, and reward power. *Legitimate power* is possessed by someone whose position (most likely in an organisational/social structure) entitles him/her to power (E.g. a policeman). Someone who has particular knowledge in a field has *expert power* over someone who does not (E.g. a medical doctor). A person who can use intimidation to elicit certain behaviour from someone else has *coercive power* over that person (E.g. a schoolyard bully). *Referent power* is possessed by someone who has earned the respect or admiration of others (E.g. a philanthropist). Finally, someone who is able to provide or withhold rewards from another person has *reward power* over that person (E.g. an employer). A person can have any number of these bases of power at any given situation.

Returning to the discussion on power distance, some authors suggest that those belonging to high power distance cultures emphasise coercive and referent power while members of low power distance cultures acknowledge legitimate and expert power (Gudykunst & Kim, 2003). Though this may generally be the case, there are variations in the power dynamics that need to be considered.

Those who are in positions of leadership in more egalitarian cultures where there is low power distance may find it difficult to understand that if they have people from high power distance cultures on their staff or under their leadership, those individuals are likely to follow the leader's directives without questioning, even if they do not agree with the leader. This understanding is crucial to a leader because, in low power distance cultures, leaders tend to assume that those under their leadership know to voice their dissent if and when necessary; and hence conclude that if someone under their leadership follows a directive that means he or she has no problem with it. But this may not necessarily be the case.

These lines of authority are further complicated when the leadership happens outside of formal organisational structures. To illustrate this further, let us consider an example. As some may be aware, a documentary called *Blindsight* (Robson-Orr & Walker, 2008) received several accolades in film festivals. The documentary chronicled the story of six blind young people from Tibet, who embarked on a climbing adventure with internationally acclaimed mountain climber, Erik Weihenmayer. Erik was the first blind man to climb Everest. The premise of the documentary is that, in response to a letter he received from the lady who runs the centre for these blind young people, Erik and his team travel to Tibet for the purpose of taking the young people on a mountain climbing adventure, under the assumption that such an adventure will imbue the children with confidence and a sense of achievement. The documentary showcases various wonderful nuances. What struck me the most as I watched the documenter, however, was that, despite genuine good intentions, Erik and his team were in a seat of power/leadership such that the children would not have had the room to decline going on the climb, if they wanted to. In other words, coming from an American perspective, Erik may have assumed that the children would share his own sense of values in terms of sense of achievement and individualism and would therefore participate in the proposed adventure as peers; while the children, arguably raised in a high power distance environment, were not in a position to contradict any plan proposed by someone in a position of leadership. The differences in these perceptions were evident in the many conversations showcased in the documentary. At a cursory glance, one might conclude that all is well that ends well, to quote the old adage. But the documentary presents much more complex and thought-provoking insights to someone who views it through the lenses of power distance and face saving.

Uncertainty Avoidance

This dimension refers to the extent to which the members of a culture are comfortable with uncertainty. Cultures high in uncertainty avoidance tend to be traditional, prefer methods that are tried and true, and prefer stability over change or even innovation. Cultures that are low in uncertainty avoidance are more prone to take risks in the pursuit of innovation and are more likely to be welcoming of strangers because interacting with strangers inherently has a measure of uncertainty.

The concept of uncertainty has been of particular interest to researchers in intercultural communication because of this element of uncertainty inherent in intercultural interactions. The argument has been made that the ability to manage the anxiety that comes with uncertainty is an asset to an intercultural communicator. One of the most widely used theories in intercultural communication is the *Anxiety/Uncertainty Management theory (AUM)* by Gudykunst (Gudykunst, 1993, 1995; Stephan, Stephan, & Gudykunst, 1999). The AUM theory is based on the premise that a basic cause for effective communication between "strangers" (people who do not belong to the same in-group) is anxiety and uncertainty management. Gudykunst (1993) extends Berger and Calabrese's (1975) *Uncertainty Reduction Theory* to intercultural contexts and argues that because intercultural encounters are novel situations, there are high levels of anxiety and uncertainty associated with them. He further argues that a person's effective communication with strangers is influenced by his/her ability to be mindful of his/her own behaviour because being mindful regulates anxiety/uncertainty management. According to Gudykunst (1993), "effective communication refers to minimising misunderstanding" (p. 34). AUM theory will be discussed in greater detail in Chapter 5. As in the other dimensions, uncertainty avoidance should also be seen as a continuum along which various cultures fall.

Conversation Break with Chris and Anusha

Anusha: I saw that once again you spent most of the class doodling on your notebook and not paying any attention!

Chris: I *was* paying attention! I just wasn't writing any notes (grins).

Anusha: Tell me again *why* you are studying diplomacy when you obviously prefer to study art?

Chris: Daddy says!

Anusha: But you're an adult, for goodness' sake! Can't you just tell your parents you're not interested in diplomacy?

Chris: I can, but I'll be letting them down. It's hard to explain. I *do* prefer to study art. But I *want* to study diplomacy as well because it means a lot to Dad for me to follow in his footsteps and I don't want to let him down.

Anusha: That sounds so weird to me. My parents don't really care what I study, as long as I do something productive with my life and do something that makes me happy.

Chris: My parents want the same thing—it's just that we have a different process for defining what's "productive" and what leads to my happiness.

Anusha: It must be like what we talked about in class—individualistic and collectivistic values.

Chris: Exactly. We see ourselves more as a collective entity I suppose. For me to become a diplomat means I honour my Dad's wishes, carry on the work he has been doing, bring honour to the extended family, etc. I don't think my parents will disown me or anything if I decide to study art, but I *want* to follow a career path that is important to them—and because it is important to them, it is important to me as I am part of them.

Anusha: That's way too deep for me at ten o'clock in the morning! But I get what you're saying. I guess I don't see myself that way as "part of" my parents—though of course I'm very loyal to them and love them. I'm my own person, you know. Their choices were good for them, now I need to make my own choices that are good for me—without letting anybody else's opinion influence my decisions.

* * *

Hofstede's dimensions of culture provide a useful framework with which to view cultural differences. However, given the extent to which globalisation has facilitated the exchange of cultural ideas, classifying whole national groups into these dimensions is not prudent. It is more helpful to think of the dimensions as values which influence behaviour. In other words, a person might behave in an individualistic way in the professional environment and behave as a collectivist when interacting with family members or friends.

Culture and Conflict Navigation

Hofestede's dimensions of culture, especially the dimensions of individualism-collectivism and power distance, have been used as frameworks with which to study conflict management. Before delving into cultural differences in attitude towards conflict as well as styles of engaging conflict, it is necessary to outline the five major styles of conflict management that are popular in conflict literature. Rahim (1983) names five styles of conflict management, arguing that each one represents varying measures of concern for self and others. The five styles are as follows:

Avoiding

This involves eluding or abstaining from engaging the person with whom there is conflict, the situation which represents potential conflict, and presumably the issues surrounding the conflict itself. Rahim argues that this style of conflict management shows low regard for self as well as for the other. According to Thiagarajan (2004), the avoidance strategy is suitable when the conflict issue is not critical, when you don't have the information needed to make an informed decision, when you are not working against a time deadline, when you know for sure that you will not be successful in getting the result you desire, or when the situation is very volatile such that it is best to allow time to pass before addressing the issue.

Obliging

Giving in to the other party's position in order to end the conflict characterises obliging. This style is seen as representative of low regard for one's self (or one's needs) and high regard for the other. This strategy is suitable when the matter of conflict is not important, when the other party has more information or expertise on the matter than you, when you know that the self-image of the other party is heavily dependent on the outcome of the conflict, when you feel you may gain a future favour from the other party by giving into their wishes this time, or when you realise that you are in the wrong (Thiagarajan, 2004).

Dominating

This style is where one party pushes for their goals to be met in the conflict situation, even using coercive means at times, without regard for the other party's wishes. Dominating is representative of high concern for one's self and low concern for the other. According to Thiagarajan, this strategy is appropriate when the issue of conflict is important, when you are sure that your point of view is correct, when you have more information or more expertise on the issue than the other party, when you feel that the other party is being manipulative, or (in situations where more than one party is involved) when you know that you have the support of the majority.

Compromising

In this process of conflict management each party gives up a little of what it wants and gets a little of what it wants. Rahim characterises compromising as a style in which there is medium concern for self and other. Compromising is the style to which people commonly defer in conflict situations, as it presents a quick and seemingly fair solution. This strategy is appropriate in situations where the issue of conflict is important, when the conflicting parties have varying expertise that is pertinent to the solution, when the conflicting parties are able to focus on the issue without taking matters personally, or when collaboration is likely to result in increased good will and future opportunities (Thiagarajan, 2004).

Integrating

This style requires a longer process of communication and negotiation in the conflict situation, as it involves getting to the deeper issues of the reason for the conflict and finding a solution that does not necessarily resemble the original proposal by each party but nevertheless satisfies the needs of both. Integrating is seen to reflect high concern for self and other.

While obliging, avoiding, and dominating are fairly self-explanatory, the difference between compromising and integrating is best illustrated by an example. Consider the situation where a beloved professor is retiring. Wishing to pay tribute to the professor, a group of students meet to discuss the manner in which they could honour her. One group suggests that they host a very grand party, inviting all the dignitaries of the university as well as alumni, soliciting special speeches from past students. The other group suggests that they should buy an expensive gift and plaque and have the latter engraved as being a gift of appreciation from that particular group of students. Having pooled their monetary resources, the students realise that they cannot throw a grand party *and* purchase an expensive gift with their limited funds. A compromise would be to throw a small party, with much fewer people in attendance, and to buy a less expensive gift with the money that is left over. It is a quick solution and, given both parties will get a close approximation of their original idea, not a bad solution at that. If the two differing groups of students were to engage in an integrating style of conflict management, however, each would ask the other the rationale behind their initial proposition. For example, the group of students who wanted to throw a grand party may say that their reason for suggesting this course of action is because they wish for their professor to be publicly honoured and for her accolades to be acclaimed as widely as possible. The group that wanted to buy the expensive gift might say that they prefer to honour the professor in a way that is more lasting than a single evening—in other words they want to give her something significant, special, and tangible, that she can keep for a long time. Thus, equating extent of "specialness" to monetary value, they wanted to buy her an expensive gift. Now that the reason behind each group's original suggestion is disclosed, the students are able to pursue alternative solutions that may satisfy the goals of both groups. As such, they could conclude that they would use their budget to hire a journalist to do an in-depth article on the professor, thus publicly honouring the professor's lifelong impact on her students, and then they would frame a clipping of the article to present to the professor as a tangible gift of special value. While the final solution which results from the process of integration does not resemble either one of the initial propositions, it does satisfy the rationale behind each one. Though not all conflict situations necessarily lend themselves to a solution through integration, and though integration is often a lengthier process than compromise, it arguably provides a more satisfactory result to all parties involved in conflict.

Communication and Conflict Navigation

One of the most widely known theories of communication in regards to conflict management is Stella Ting-Toomey's *Face Negotiation Theory* (Ting-Toomey, 1988; 1993), which addresses cultural variations in conflict management through various facework tactics. Our face, or public image, is rendered vulnerable in conflict situations. Face encompasses not only our image but also our identity, honour, and self-esteem. Ting-Toomey and Oetzel (2002) explain:

> *Self-face* is the concern for one's own image, and *other-face* is the concern for another's image. Although most prior research has focused only on these two loci of face, a third concern, mutual-face, is also relevant. *Mutual-face* is the concern for both parties' images and/or the "image" of the relationship (p. 145).

We often use facework to save self-face, other-face, and mutual-face. Facework strategies include tact, approbation, and solidarity (Lim & Bowers, 1991).

Tact

This strategy involves respecting another person's autonomy and preventing them from losing face. For example, if your boss who usually presents a strong front to everyone receives some bad news and breaks down in tears, you may, knowing he would be embarrassed if he knew someone was watching, pretend to look the other way. Tact is a strategy that is usually used to preserve other-face. Consider another example of the use of tact. Suppose an employee asks an employer for a flexible work schedule due to personal reasons. Not knowing whether these reasons may be embarrassing and may cause the employee to lose face if s/he were asked to specify them, but needing to know more information in order to be able to determine whether flexible hours can be provided, the employer could use tact by asking the employee to specify how s/he intends to make up for lost hours, should a personal emergency arise. This way the employee is able to provide the information related to work hours that the employer needs, without having to reveal the personal reasons for the request for flexible hours.

Approbation

This facework tactic involves focusing on the positive aspects or merits of the other person instead of the negative. For example, if you are to chide an employee regarding an error he made, and knowing that conversation would cause him to lose face, you may start by highlighting that he is a meticulous worker and suggesting he must have had an-off day as an error of that kind isn't indicative of usual work. By minimising the focus on assigning blame and maximising the focus on recognising the other person's merits, approbation serves as a useful strategy to save other-face.

Solidarity

This involves identifying with the other person in some way to create a sense that both of you belong to the same ingroup. Solidarity can be a useful technique in establishing an amiable conversational platform before discussing an issue of conflict, thus saving mutual-face. For example, if you want to approach a colleague about a project for which both of you have missed the deadline, you could use solidarity by starting with an acknowledgement that you have both been very busy and you understand how it's possible to let something slip, thus inviting the other person into your ingroup before bringing up the issue that could potentially lead to loss of face for one or both parties.

* * *

One of the assumptions on which *Face Negotiation Theory* is based is that conflict management is mediated by culture and face. Generally speaking, it appears that low context individualistic cultures prefer dominating and integrating styles of conflict management while high context collectivistic cultures prefer obliging, avoiding, or compromising styles (West & Turner, 2004). There are, however, subtle differences in national groups. For example, in a study involving U.S. Americans, Chinese, Koreans, Taiwanese and Japanese, Ting-Toomey et al. (1991) found that Taiwanese, Chinese and Americans used domination more than Japanese and Koreans. Further, Chinese used avoiding more than the other national groups in the study and Japanese used compromising more than the other groups (these were reported use of conflict styles as opposed to observed use). In a later study with different ethnic groups in the United States, Ting-Toomey et al. (2000) found that the participants who identified strongly with the individualistic values of the American culture in general tended to use integration and compromise more than those whose cultural identity was weak.

The differences in preference of style of conflict management may be indicative of cultural differences in attitude towards conflict itself. Those who see conflict as a positive and natural part of relationship development, see it as something to be engaged, processed and overcome, assuming that the relationship will be stronger for having gone through the process of conflict. Those who see conflict in a negative light see it as a threat to relationship and therefore try every possible means to avoid it or diffuse it quickly in order to maintain (or restore) harmony in the relationship. Ting-Toomey & Oetzel (2002) write:

> In individualistic cultures, there may be more communication situations that evoke the need for independent-based decisions and behaviours. In group-based cultures, there may be more situations that demand the sensitivity for interdependent-based decisions and actions. The manner in which individuals conceive of their self-images—independent versus interdependent selves—in a particular conflict situation should have a profound influence on what type of facework behaviours and conflict styles they would use in a conflict episode (p. 145).

The general preference of individualistic cultures toward low context mode of communication also facilitates a confrontational approach to conflict where emotions and frustrations can be vocalised in a linear communication exchange. Being oriented to subtlety and nonverbal-contextual means of communication, high context communicators may be less inclined to verbalise the issue of conflict. As discussed earlier, a person of collectivistic values is trained to think in terms of the group or dyad (as the case may be) and make decisions accordingly while an individualistic person largely assumes responsibility for his/her own actions and expects the other person to do the same. Given this, it is reasonable to imagine that, in a conflict situation between two such individuals, the collectivist would think of employing facework to save face for self and other while the individualist may not feel the responsibility to save the other's face (again, with the assumption that the other person is responsible for saving his/her own face). Consider the following example, which illustrates an interaction between Dr. Cook, a lecturer who has collectivistic values, and Eric, a student with individualistic values.

Dr. Cook is a lecturer assigned to teach a class in Communication to undergraduate students. As is common in any university class, some students did very well in her classes while others did not. Eric belonged to the latter group of students. He scraped a pass in the first test, and barely missed the pass mark on the second one. Towards the end of the semester, after receiving a failing mark on the third test, Eric storms up to Dr. Cook's office and vents his frustration.

"I can't believe I failed another test! I can't afford to fail this class because I intend to graduate next semester!" he exclaims.

"I can understand why that would be upsetting, Eric," responds Dr. Cook. But I am wondering why you did not speak with me when you failed the second test. Perhaps then I could have helped you work out what you could've done differently to perform better on the third one."

"This is the only class I'm having trouble in!" responds Eric. "I do well in all my other classes," he continues in a raised voice, nearly yelling. "I think I'm doing badly because *you* don't know how to write exam questions!"

"Well, clearly you are an intelligent student if you are doing well in your other classes. Do you think you studied sufficiently and familiarised yourself with all the readings and class notes before the test?" asks Dr. Cook, maintaining a calm tone.

"I did the best I could, OK? It's the end of the semester, there's tons to do and I don't have time to go over every little detail in every class. Your questions are so unfair! Nobody has that kind of time to study every little thing! And nobody has three tests in a class on top of a group project! That's just insane! You should give us the option to drop the lowest test mark. That's the fair thing to do."

"The end of the semester can be a tough time. It's a busy time even for us lecturers, so I understand the pressure you must be feeling. But I don't demand of you any more than I demand of your colleagues; and you were aware of all the requirements of this class from the beginning of the semester. Had you spoken to me when you failed the first test, I would have been able to help you by explaining the concepts with which you may have had trouble. But it is difficult to address something that's already done. You're clearly confident and bold; as I'm sure it takes a courageous student to directly express his concerns to a lecturer as you've just done. So I suggest that you use that confidence to apply yourself fully to the group project that's due next week. If you get a high enough mark, you may still pass the class," says Dr. Cook, in a polite but firm tone which indicates that the conversation is over.

Eric uses a very direct style of communication in this example. He verbalises his thoughts, leaving little room for ambiguity. He confines to defending his own face (by providing excuses for why he failed the test and re-directing blame on the lecturer) and openly threatens the face of the lecturer by accusing her of being unfair and inept at writing exams. Dr. Cook, on the other hand, uses facework strategies to save Eric's face as well as her own. She uses approbation when she compliments Eric for being "clearly intelligent" and bold. She uses solidarity when explaining that she understands how busy the end of the semester could be. She defends her own face when she explains that she is not asking something unique of Eric that she hasn't asked of the other students. Being the person who had the seat of power in this interaction, Dr. Cook could have cut the conversation short by asking Eric to leave till he could speak more respectfully or simply saying that two consecutive failures are indicative of lack of preparation or lack of competency on the student's part. Either one of these responses would have effectively ended the conversation. However, they would have caused Eric to lose face. Instead Dr. Cook chooses to engage in a longer conversation which avoids loss of face for Eric while holding firmly to her position in the argument. This example is presented not only to illustrate the use of facework to save one's face as well as the other's but also to convey that facework strategies can be effectively used to diffuse a potentially volatile situation.

Like individualism-collectivism, the cultural dimension of power distance also appears to influence conflict management. There is limited evidence to suggest that managers are likely to involve their peers and subordinates in the process of conflict resolution in low power distance cultures (Smith et al., 1998). Kaushal and Kwantes (2006) use the concept of vertical and horizontal individualism-collectivism to further explain differences in conflict management style in regards to power differences:

> A high score in the vertical collectivism dimension implies that even within a 'group-oriented' culture, there is still an awareness of individual needs. . . . A similar examination of the horizontal individualism and collectivism constructs reveal a high concern for the other and a low concern for the self, respectively, as the former is indicative of strong emphasis on the collective and the latter suggests a focus on the group beyond that of the individual. Thus, the former would be more likely to result in an integrating or obliging style of conflict resolution, whereas the latter would more often lead to obliging or avoiding (p. 583).

Encounters between persons from high and low power distance cultures, especially in a professional setting like in today's multicultural organisations, can cause conflict. Chong (2006) explains, for example, that in the Korean culture (which is higher in power distance than many Western cultures) it is not uncommon for someone in a lower social status (by age, organisational hierarchy, etc.) to oblige to the person of a higher social status, even when it comes to playing a game of golf. The person of lesser status would concede that the other person has scored appropriately even if that was not the case, merely to save face for the person of higher status. Given many a business deal is sealed over a game of golf, the implications of a golf game between a Korean businessman who considers himself of a higher social status (perhaps due to age) and a younger Westernised businessman are interesting to consider!

Within a higher power distance culture itself, however, multiple styles of conflict management may be used. For example, Zhang (2007) found that in Chinese families which adopted a conversation-oriented style of parenting, collaborative styles of conflict management and compromises were typical, while in families where parents used a conformation-oriented style of parenting, avoidance was a common form of conflict management.

The concept of "culture" inherently lends itself to the ingroup—outgroups distinction which is often an essential ingredient in conflict. Worchel (2005) proposes that any threat to cultural values and traditions, which are a vital part of our social identity, perpetuate conflict. He goes on to argue that the rapid change in technology and social configurations of societies (due to migration patterns) is contributing to uncertainty and threatens cultural identities, thus setting the platform for conflict. There is also great fear incited by acts of terrorism as well as violent environmental phenomena. As a means of justifying fear, it is tempting to assign blame to particular cultural groups as being instigators or contributors to the causes of fear. Looking back at how we collectively construct the social structures within which we confine our lives, it is evident that the solution to today's "state of fear" also lies in collective effort. The vilification of any one group of people is a simplistic and irresponsible solution to the status quo to which we have collectively contributed. Oetzel and colleagues (2007) point out that many external interventions to solve community-level conflicts such as in the case of Somalia are unsuccessful because of the lack of involvement of the local group in the conflict management strategy. This reiterates the significance of collective ownership of the solution to conflict.

To further illustrate the importance of considering cultural realities in conflict management, an example is considered here based on a Christian teaching of conflict management. This approach is chosen because Christian values are integrated into many Westernised cultures, implicitly or explicitly. One of the foundational texts used as a teaching on conflict management comes from the book of Mathew, in which Jesus is recorded saying:

> If a fellow believer hurts you, go and tell him—work it out between the two of you. If he listens, you've made a friend. If he won't listen, take one or two others along so that the presence of witnesses will keep things honest, and try again. (Matt 18:15 – 16, Message Bible).

Unpacking this teaching in general terms, it can be said that the procedure to follow if someone offends you is to discuss the matter directly with the person concerned, if s/he won't listen, then bring a friend into the conversation. Of course, this verse is presented in the context of those who subscribe to the Christian faith. However, the practice of direct confrontation and the philosophy of "if you have a problem with me tell me to my face," are not unfamiliar to most. The practice of involving a mediator is also not uncommon. So let us consider the first two steps of the outlined process: 1) Address the issue directly with the other party. 2) Involve a mediator or two, if the conflict is not resolved by the first step. Generally speaking, this approach to conflict management seems entirely reasonable and practical. However, it is prudent to reflect on how this process may be played out in light of cultural differences.

The first step outlined is the direct confrontation. In cultures where linear, low context mode of communication is common practice, direct confrontation is just that—a conversation between the conflicting parties, specifically addressing the issue of conflict. However, in cultures where face saving and maintaining relational harmony are high priorities, the first step might look quite different. Addressing the matter of conflict directly with the other party may not involve a conversation about the issue of conflict at all. It may in fact be a meeting in which the parties concerned share a meal and talk about topics of mutual interest. However, the very act of sharing a meal involves one person arranging to have the meal with the other, the other person accepting the invitation to spend time, and both parties sharing the same space and participating in an act of socialisation in the midst of conflict. In the conversation, there may be indirect references to the matter of conflict without explicitly discussing the issue itself. But the message that is conveyed is relational—the act of sharing the meal says that both parties care enough about the relationship in order to spend time doing something that only friends do. It is not unlike the intended message behind a direct confrontation, which can be construed as one party's concern for the relationship such that s/he is willing to brave the unpleasantness of a conversation about the conflict in order to save the friendship.

The second step of involving a mediator might also look quite different in different cultural contexts. Often in Westernised cultures, the mediator is a neutral party, someone who is acceptable to both parties concerned but exclusively affiliated with neither—or it could be someone closely affiliated with both parties, someone trusted by both. In other cultural contexts the mediator could very well be someone who is closer to one party than the other, once again whose presence in the conversation conveying the message louder than an explicit discussion about the issue of conflict. The point to remember, then, is that even though in theory the procedure of settling the matter between the conflicting parties and/or involving a mediator is straightforward and arguably effective, the practical outworking of it might vary depending on cultural context. This matter is of particular importance to those in positions of leadership of multicultural organisations in which they may have to provide advice to members involved in conflicts. If the conflicting parties are from cultures where high context and implicit styles of communication are practiced, then the leader must remember that s/he should not insist that the conflicting parties "hash it out face to face" or "clear the air" in the way linear communicators would. The advice to address the matter directly with the other party is possibly a sound one, as long as the leader bears in mind that this process may not involve a direct explicit conversation about the issue of conflict.

Strategies for Healthy Communication in Conflict

There is a vast body of literature which addresses the topic of conflict exclusively and provides both frameworks for understanding conflict as well as strategies for managing conflict situations (Wilmot & Hocker, 2007, for example). Though this chapter is not intended to provide a comprehensive take on intercultural conflict, it is helpful to identify a few practical measures one can take to facilitate healthy intercultural communication in situations of conflict.

Maintain Contact

It is natural to wish to withdraw from the person with whom you perceive conflict. However, by doing so you disconnect yourself from the primary and most reliable source of information about the conflict, which is the other person. When two conflicting parties cease communication with each other, they have to rely on secondary sources to find out the other party's claims, intentions, proposed actions, etc. The secondary sources may or may not be reliable. For example, in interpersonal conflict between friends, the conflicting parties may rely on mutual friends to provide them with information about how the other person is feeling. But mutual friends may not relay the information accurately due to their own emotional involvement in the situation, and due to the normal process of filtering the information through their own perceptual processes. I must, however, acknowledge that in cultures highly attuned to facework, the involvement of a mutually respected third party is a normal part of maintaining contact with the other conflicting party. In such cases, the conflicting parties must be extra vigilant in selecting a mediator who is both qualified and trusted by all parties to accurately represent their points of view.

In a conflict between two companies, to consider another example, if direct communication is ceased then the companies have to rely on the media for information about the intentions of the other company, and, once again, this information may not be precise. Therefore it is advisable to maintain close contact with the other conflicting parties as much as possible.

Assume Best Intentions

In intercultural situations, the potential opportunities for conflict and misunderstanding are high due to the cultural differences that add a layer of complexity to the communication. If someone behaves in what we perceive to be an offensive manner, it is good practice to first assume that the behaviour was the result of a cultural misunderstanding rather than malicious intent. It is possible that this assumption turns out to be erroneous, but at least this state of mind would provide an opportunity to investigate the reason behind the perceived offence further and possibly diffuse any conflict before it happens.

It was discussed in Chapter 1 that the most common form of attribution error is the Fundamental Attribution Error. The opportunities to commit a FAE are high in conflict situations. In interpersonal conflict, it is easy to assume that the reason for the other person's behaviour is based on his/her personality. For example, you may assume, "He's insisting on resolving this his way because he's stubborn." But it is possible that the reason for the other person's assertive behaviour is circumstantial (perhaps he would lose his job if the outcome of the conflict does not turn out in his favour) rather than a factor of his personality. We may not have unequivocal proof as to whether our initial assumptions about the other party are correct—but if we start by assuming that the other party is acting in good faith, then our own disposition will be conducive for being open to listen to all relevant perspectives.

Provide a Safe Platform

When seeking clarification about a perceived slight or offence, adapt a style of communication which provides a safe platform for the other person to explain their intentions. In other words, if you ask a question aggressively or in a confrontational manner, the other person might feel threatened or offended and either respond aggressively in turn or withdraw from the conversation. This would not facilitate the process of understanding the reason behind the initial behaviour that lead to the conflict. Going back to the previous point about assuming best intentions, if you assume that the other person did not intend to offend, then you are likely to ask for clarification in a friendly manner that is conducive for a friendly response.

Often issues of conflict persist over a prolonged period due to lack of information and lack of candid communication between the conflicting parties. This lack of communication may be due to the fact that one or more parties do not feel safe to be vulnerable with the other party, either due to their own insecurities or due to past experiences where information they had shared during moments of vulnerability was used as ammunition against them. Though you may not have control over someone else's insecurities, you do have control over how you treat their moments of vulnerability. By consistently behaving in a trustworthy and discreet manner, you provide a safe platform for the other person to communicate candidly. Establishing this trustworthy manner involves maintaining confidentiality of thoughts shared by the other person (unless the other person gives permission for the information to be shared with another party), refraining from personal attacks on the other person, and refraining from reacting defensively when the other person shares his/her feelings of hurt that may have resulted from your behaviour. Often a defensive response to someone's grievance is to point out the ways in which they have hurt you.

For example, assume that a husband says to his wife, "I feel hurt when you tell our friends in public that I'm not a good cook." Assume that the wife responds by saying, "Well, you hurt my feelings too, when you tell people I can't drive!" In this exchange, the wife's response is defensive—instead of listening to the hurt expressed by her husband, she is reacting defensively by pointing out that he too is an offender. Such a response implies that the husband has no right to bring up this offence because he is not perfect. But it is an unhelpful response because neither party's point of view is satisfactorily heard. Instead of responding to the husband's grievance by bringing up a grievance of her own, if the wife responds by saying, "I'm sorry. I didn't realise you feel that way. I was only joking—I didn't mean to hurt your feelings," then the husband would feel heard (especially if she follows up these words by refraining from publicly jibing her husband in the future!). Such a response not only provides a safe platform for future communication, but also facilitates the husband's own disposition to hear the wife's grievances when the time is appropriate. It is important to recognise that if your first response is defensive whenever the other party tries to communicate his/her grievances, then the other person would eventually cease to communicate, as you have not provided a safe platform for this communication. Thus providing a safe platform for communication is vital for healthy communication during conflict.

Involve a Mediator

It is appropriate at times to involve a third party mediator who is either neutral (this is appropriate in a conflict situation between two companies, for example) or equally intimate with and trusted by both parties (this is appropriate in conflict situations between friends or members of the family). The third party mediator can be especially helpful in intercultural conflict situations, particularly if s/he understands both cultures well and is able to explain to the conflicting parties the cultural norms that each one should understand and/or adopt in order to facilitate reconciliation.

The involvement of a mediator is particularly appropriate if there are sensitive face issues involved in the conflict. For example, you may be a person in a position of authority in a high power distance culture. You may have a conflict issue that needs to be addressed with someone who is a subordinate. If you directly confront the person, you know that the person would lose face. Hence you may recruit the help of another person who is trusted by both parties, and who is of equal position with your subordinate, to gently bring up the issue of conflict with the subordinate. By doing so, you allow your subordinate to save face by not having to discuss the matter directly with you, a person in a position of higher power.

Involving a mediator is also appropriate when the issue of conflict is highly emotional and it is impossible for the conflicting parties to communicate directly with each other in a helpful manner. In such a situation, a trusted mediator who is not as emotionally invested as the conflicting parties would be able to facilitate the communication for the achievement of an amicable resolution. Further, if the conflicting parties are from different cultures and lack the necessary information to comprehend the other party's point of view, a mediator who is familiar with both cultural perspectives could facilitate effective communication.

Consider the Relationship

Conflict may result due to perceived incompatibility of goals, values, ideas, emotions, etc. Ultimately, however, there is a relationship at stake in any conflict situation, specifically the relationship between the conflicting parties. The question one has to ask one's self is whether the cause of the conflict is worth the cost of the relationship.

Ideally, the conflict would be resolved through one of the strategies of conflict resolution. However, if a conflict persists without hope for resolution, one has to weigh the cost and determine whether holding one's position is worth losing the relationship with the other party.

It is a serious matter to consider. It is possible that one might arrive at the conclusion that the reason behind the conflict is indeed worthy of pursuit, no matter the cost. However, it is important to pause to consider the relationship at stake in a conflict situation because often the conflicting parties are too distracted by the issue of conflict that they do not realise that they may be paying a higher price in losing their relationship while standing up for an issue that may not be as significant to them in the long run.

Further, sometimes it takes one party to concede their point at the expense of losing face in order to resolve the conflict. It is good to consider the value of the relationship if you are faced with such a situation so that you can weigh whether the relationship is of more value than a temporary loss of face. It is also helpful to pause to consider the repercussions of this particular conflict on relationships outside of the conflicting parties. For example, the conflict may be between two friends, but others who are friends with both conflicting parties are often caught in the middle and suffer the tensions of the conflict as well. Pausing to consider the relationships that may be affected by your conflict enables you to see the larger implications of this particular conflict and gives you the appropriate frame of mind for healthy communication with the other party.

Consider Moving On

As mentioned earlier, the ideal situation in a conflict is that the matter would be resolved to the satisfaction of both parties. However, sometimes due to unavoidable circumstances, external pressures, or the immaturity of the persons involved, a matter of conflict cannot be resolved. Prolonged conflict causes relational deterioration. Sometimes it is wise to let go of the issue (and possibly the relationship) and move on.

Though this is may not be the ideal solution, it may be the healthier one overall because conflict between two parties does not occur in a social vacuum. Relational conflicts often affect others who are emotionally tied to the conflicting parties. As mentioned in the previous point, it is important to consider the relationships that are affected by a particular conflict and choose one's actions accordingly. Prolonged conflict can cause strain in relationships between people who are not directly involved in the particular issue of conflict. Hence, in situations where it seems that sustained efforts have proved unfruitful in resolving the conflict, consider moving on.

"Moving on" might involve obliging, avoiding, compromising beyond what you had initially hoped, or merely letting go of a relationship if it is the cause of prolonged and destructive conflict. The latter is of course an extreme measure and one that may not be an option in some kinds of relationships. The point to note, however, is that disengagement from conflict is sometimes the healthiest communication strategy.

Though it is unwise to be dogmatically prescriptive when it comes to communication practices, it is nevertheless helpful to consider some specific strategies like the ones discussed in this section to foster healthy patterns of communication in conflict. It is also helpful to be particularly mindful of the added complexity of deep-seated cultural values, when navigating conflict in intercultural spaces.

Chapter Four
CULTURAL TRANSITION AND ADAPTATION

Those of us who have had the opportunity to travel and experience new cultures have also experienced the feeling of exhilaration mixed with disorientation and frustration that comes from the unfamiliarity of a new cultural environment. There is much research on the phenomena of cultural transition, adaptation, acculturation, and migration, due to their relevance in today's highly mobile societies. Many younger countries such as the United States, Australia, Canada, and the United Kingdom are largely made up of immigrant populations which contribute to the social richness as well as a measure of confusion of cultural identity in the nation. From the basic individual-level factors to the larger global implications, understanding the process of cultural transition is a necessary part of understanding communication in intercultural spaces.

One of the terms that is often used in discussions of migration and cultural transition, is globalisation. *Globalisation* is so frequently used in various contexts that its meaning has become somewhat pliable. Berry (2008) sees globalisation as a process, and describes it as,

> a complex process, rather than to the kinds of outcomes, which take place when societies engage in international contact. This process involves a flow of cultural elements (ideas, goods etc.), and the establishing of relationships and networks. It does not specify what societies and their individual members do in response to this process, nor identify the changes that take place among them (p. 330).

Another conceptualisation of globalisation comes from Inda and Rosaldo (2006), who describe globalisation as consisting of

> spatial-temporal processes, operating on a global scale that rapidly cut across national boundaries, drawing more and more of the world into webs of interconnection, integrating and stretching cultures and communities across space and time, and compressing our spatial and temporal horizons (p. 9).

Again, this definition also portrays globalisation as a process rather than a set of outcomes. On the one hand globalisation has researchers concerned about the survival of indigenous cultures (Bhawuk, 2008), while on the other hand researchers recognise the paradoxical situation where globalisation elicits feelings of territoriality and allegiance to traditional ways of life (Salzman, 2008). While the society as a whole grapples with the implications of globalisation, the individual goes through his/her own process of transition, acculturation, and negotiation of cultural identity. It is this individual process that is of particular interest to a student of intercultural communication. Thus the appropriate place to start this discussion of cultural transition is at the individual level, starting with what one experiences upon first exposure to a new cultural environment.

Culture Shock

The phrase *culture shock* is widely used to describe the feeling of disorientation and discomfort that are common when encountering a new culture. Feelings of homesickness, hostility toward the new culture, mild depression, and over-identification with home culture typify culture shock.

One of my own comical (in retrospect!) encounters with culture shock occurred a couple of months after I first arrived as a student in the United States. I had just landed a part-time job in the university cafeteria, and headed over to start my first day on the job with excitement about my imminent affluence. Nothing in my entire nineteen years (during which time I had already lived in two other countries) had prepared me for what I was about to face on that day.

The cafeteria supervisor brusquely explained the various workstations, pointed out that I should at all times cover my hair and wear gloves while handling food, and instructed me to assist with frying chicken fingers, filling drink orders, and manning (womaning?) the cash register (which involved checking students' IDs to ensure they were in possession of their own meal cards).

By the time I had donned the appropriate attire and oriented myself to the stations, it was lunch hour. Crowds of students started gathering and shouting out various orders. I tried to listen intently and figure out what each one was asking (as I had trouble deciphering the accents) while not getting in the way of the frenzy of activity all around me. Some yelled for a "large Hawaiian punch." I had no idea what that could be! Someone else held up their ID and rapidly placed his order while I squinted at the picture and then back at the person to figure out if it was the same face. To my untrained eye, all the white faces looked the same. Another person handed me a five dollar note and waited for change. I tried to calculate the change I owed her (the supervisor had neglected to show me that the cash register was capable of calculating the change on its own) while trying to distinguish between the various silver coins, none of which looked familiar.

Meanwhile the line of people was getting longer and longer. I caught the supervisor's eye and yelled in desperation, "There's a long queue!" and received a blank stare in response. After repeating this plea a few times I realised that the supervisor did not understand me, but I had no idea why. Later, much later, I discovered that the British colonial influence in my upbringing had prompted me to use the word "queue" when I should have said "line" instead, which is the word with which Americans are familiar.

My career in the university cafeteria was quite short-lived. In an attempt to salvage the remains of my dignity, I resigned at the end of my shift before the supervisor had the chance to fire me.

Culture shock and the adaptation that (hopefully!) follows are described in the theoretical concept of the *U-curve*. According to the U-curve framework, there are three phases to cultural transition. At the top of the U is the *honeymoon* phase in which a person is quite excited at the prospect of experiencing a new culture and finds everything novel and interesting. Soon, the emotions begin to take a downward slide down the U, and one hits the *crisis* phase where homesickness, disorientation, and frustrations culminate into an all-time low point in the sojourner's experience. With increasing familiarity with the new culture, however, the person regains confidence and familiarity and once more reaches the top of the U in the *adaptation* phase, where all is well in the new culture which is now no longer "new." The U-curve model does not offer a timeframe for each one of its stages but merely suggests that, given enough time, a sojourner is likely to experience the different stages of the model. Oberg (1960), who is credited for coining the phrase culture shock, describes the feelings characteristic of this phenomenon:

> A feeling of helplessness and a desire for dependence on long-term residents of one's own nationality; fits of anger over delays and other minor frustrations; delay and outright refusal to learn the language of the host country; excessive fear of being cheated, robbed, or injured; . . . terrible longing to be home . . . and, in general, talk to people who really make sense (p. 176).

Those who successfully adapt to a new culture are those who intentionally engage the members of the host culture, participate in formalised social networks (such as clubs, places of worship, interest groups, etc.), and are generally open to other cultural worldviews. In my own experience, I discovered that forming friendships with other sojourners was an easier first step to forming friendships with host nationals. As an international student in the USA, I first befriended students from various other countries who were also experiencing homesickness and disorientation as I was, found solidarity and comfort in the fact that I wasn't alone, and then felt bold enough to engage American students who somehow seemed to be quite different from the other international students, despite the fact that the latter group was hardly homogenous.

The *W-curve* (two U curves put together) illustrates the process of re-entry. When a sojourner is preparing to return home, he might be very excited, looking forward to all the familiar experiences of "home" with fond memories and hoping to share the new insights he has learned from his travels, with his friends and family. Upon return, however, the sojourner discovers that time has elapsed in his absence, his friends have had new shared experiences that did not include him, and possibly they are neither interested in nor capable of understanding the new insights he has had from being exposed to a different cultural environment. At this point the returning sojourner might experience discouragement, loneliness, and "homesickness" for the country of sojourn. As time passes, however, the process of recovery once again takes place and the sojourner adjusts back to the home culture. Thus, the W-curve depicts the first U of the experience with the new culture and the second U of the experience of returning to the home culture.

Though the U and W curves may be simplistic representations of the complex process of cultural transition, they provide helpful and accessible frameworks with which to understand the experiences associated with culture shock and eventual acculturation.

Acculturation

Acculturation as a topic of study has drawn the interest of researchers in fields such as communication, psychology, and sociology, largely due to its relevance in today's society. Chirkov (2009) makes the argument that most of the research in acculturation has been from a positivistic social scientific perspective and contends that these are not the best approaches from which to study acculturation because the subject matter involves the study of cultural processes. A positivistic approach to research is based on the assumption that knowledge can be accessed through our senses and therefore positivistic research is based on empirical observations (Anderson, 1996). Nevertheless, great strides have been made in acculturation research in recent times.

Berry (2005) defines acculturation as, "the dual process of cultural and psychological change that takes place as a result of contact between two or more cultural groups and their individual members" (p. 698). Intercultural contact brings about change not only in the individual but also in the collective social context in which the contact occurs. One has only to observe the food choices in an everyday mall food court over a period of years to recognise the influence of intercultural contact. The presence of kebabs and samosas in a food court in Sydney Australia illustrates this point just as effectively as the presence of Big Macs in a food court in Colombo Sri Lanka. From food to music to fashion, the influence of one culture on another brought about by globalisation is evident over the years.

Unlike assimilation, which is the process whereby a migrant completely embraces the practices and cultural identity of the new culture, acculturation can vary in its outcome, depending on the choices made by the migrant. One of the widely known theoretical frameworks which describe the process of acculturation is Berry's boxes (Berry, 1980; Berry et al., 1989) in which four acculturation choices are identified, namely integration, assimilation, separation, and marginalisation.

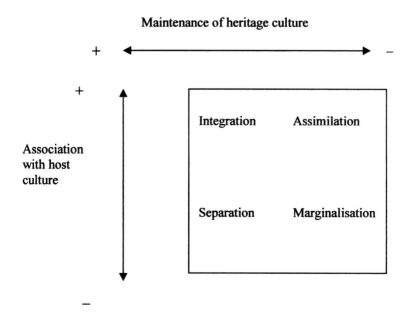

Maintenance of heritage culture

Figure: Berry's model of acculturation (Adapted from Berry, 2005)

The state of *marginalisation* or alienation refers to the situation where a migrant has negative attitudes toward both home and host culture, thus feeling excluded and not quite belonging to either culture. When a migrant has a positive attitude toward home culture but a negative attitude toward the host culture, this state is called *separation*. Migrants in the state of separation often associate only with other migrants from the home culture and do not interact with members of the host culture unless it is necessary on a functional basis. *Assimilation* characterises the situation where a migrant has a negative attitude towards the home culture and positive attitude towards the host culture, thus fully embracing the ways of the host culture while relinquishing the home culture's ways. Finally, *integration* refers to the state where a migrant has positive attitudes towards both home and host culture and successfully integrates the ways of both in the process of acculturation. While these acculturation strategies are described from the point of view of the migrant, Berry (2005) also identifies four corresponding labels from the perspective of the host culture, namely multiculturalism (integration), melting pot (assimilation), segregation (separation) and exclusion (marginalisation).

In a study of Sri Lankan Tamil immigrants in Australia, Arasaratnam (2008) used Berry's model as a framework for understanding the choices made by the immigrants. One could argue that people who migrate under political duress may be prone to separation rather than voluntary migrants, based on the rationale that voluntary migrants *choose* their new home while political refugees may not have chosen to leave their home country had it not been for conditions of duress. The study, however, found that those who migrated voluntarily in pursuit of economic prosperity or family reunion were the ones who were prone to separation, while those who migrated under political duress were prone to integration. This is an interesting finding because it provides a glimpse into the psyche of the category of immigrant who is an asylum-seeker or a political refugee, as the participants who fit in this category expressed that they wanted to integrate with the host society and contribute to its prosperity because they were grateful for the refuge they had been provided. Those who chose migration voluntarily, on the other hand, expressed that they preferred to maintain the roots of their home culture by living in diasporas (communities of migrants who retain the home cultural identity, often due to the lack of recognition or place for that identity in the mainstream host culture) where they can retain their cultural identity without much mingling with the host culture. The study further found that children of first generation migrants either fell into the category of marginalisation or assimilation.

Berry's model of acculturation is not without its critics. Some researchers express concern that models of acculturation such as Berry's don't take into account the complex element of cultural identity which is intricately related to the process of acculturation. For example, Weinreich (2009) states:

> In further commenting on Berry's model, note that a close association between the culture of a group and the identity of individuals of the group is often assumed, as in heritage culture and ethnic identity. 'Culture' is incorporated as personal interpretations of various cultural manifestations into personal identity as aspects of the person's biographical experiences. In effect, culture and identity are intricately related, so that for people to reject their heritage culture would be to reject the cultural aspects of their identity heritage (p. 125).

From Weinreich's perspective, this is a problematic conceptualisation. He goes on to suggest that *enculturation* is the more salient variable, not acculturation. Weinreich posits that enculturation "references the agentic individual's process of identification with whatever cultural elements of influential others are available to that person" (p. 127) and goes on to explain that when a person moves to a different culture, this process of enculturation continues (at the identity level), only this time it is complicated by encounters with individuals whose culture is different from the individual's own. Weinreich argues that looking at the immigrant's experience in terms of choices to reject or accept host/home cultures (as suggested in Berry's model) does not take into account this key process of identity formation.

Bhatia and Ram (2009) suggests that a better understanding of the migrant's experiences can be achieved by studying diasporas instead of focusing on the migrant's individual acculturative choices. Having studied the Indian Diaspora in the United States especially after the events of 9/11, Bhatia and Ram argue that key events in the host culture play a large role in shaping the identity of immigrant communities; a process that isn't reflected in the linear approaches to the study of acculturation (such as in Berry's model). The authors suggest that

> Although integration and bicultural competency may be worthy goals to achieve, . . . for most people living in contemporary diasporas, their negotiation with multiple cultural sites is fluid, dynamic, interminable and often unstable. Achieving integration may simply not be an option and/or may be achieved temporarily only to be lost at some point and so on. The acculturation journey is not a teleological trajectory that has a fixed end-point but instead has to be continuously negotiated (p. 148).

Berry's model of acculturation views the process from the perspective of the migrant and the choices he or she makes. As the model depicts, the migrant's choices are characterised in terms of levels of affiliation with host and home culture. Rudmin (2009) suggests that acculturation should instead be studied and defined in terms of second-culture acquisition. Instead of defining acculturation in terms of change in one's culture (which has connotations of marginalisation of minority groups); Rudmin argues that it should be viewed as learning an "alien" culture.

Social Value

A concept that merits further discussion is the notion of *social value*. There are many challenges a migrant faces, such as adjusting to new cultural norms, finding employment, familiarising one's self with the geographical as well as social landscape of the new home and so on. In addition to all of this, a migrant has to contend with establishing social value in the new culture. Social value can be defined as the perception of the worth of a person based on pre-established societal criteria of social currency. For example, in many high power distant cultures, social norms dictate that older people should be treated with deference and respect. This means, in such cultures, a person's social value arguably increases with age. In cultures that revere youthfulness, however, an older person will have less social value based on that particular criterion. To illustrate with another example, in cultures that value education, a highly educated person is of more social value compared to someone who isn't, regardless of the amount of money possessed by each one of these persons. In other cultures, one's wealth is of significant social value such that it compensates for the lack of one's accomplishments in other areas.

When a person migrates to a new culture, (unless he/she already has previously established relationships with people in that culture) he/she is anonymous for a certain period of time, until relationships are established. During this period of time the migrant has to contend with a state where his/her social value is also being established. If a person moves from one city to another within the same country, even though he/she would still have to make new friends and establish new social networks, at least the migrant would be aware of the specifics that form the social currency of that particular country and would have a sense of how he/she would be received by new acquaintances. But this is not the case when someone moves to an entirely new country. Establishing social value in a new country presents unique challenges which may not be obvious to one unless one has personally experienced this process. Perhaps these challenges are best illustrated through an example.

Consider Wes and Grace, a retired couple in their early sixties, who decide to migrate to a different country to be near their children and grandchildren. Though their children help them settle into a convenient apartment and provide for their expenses, Wes and Grace still find themselves having to establish their own social network of friends in the new country. Coming from a high power distant, masculine society, Wes is used to having high social value where, being a highly educated older man, he had a position of status and respect in his community. Having been an accountant for more than thirty years in the same town, Wes was well-known in the community and wherever he went he received the royal treatment from past clients, colleagues, and others who had known him for many years. Grace had always been a stay at home wife and was content with her life. Her social value was intricately associated with that of Wes, and she too was treated with respect wherever she went, given she was Wes' wife. When they moved to the new country, things change.

Suddenly Wes and Grace find themselves in a society where youthfulness was more valued than age, and therefore they no longer have inherent social value due to their age. In fact, the fact that they are older and retired immediately puts them in what appears to be an "obsolete" category. Further, Wes begins to realise that Grace was making friends easier and getting invited to more social gatherings because she is more conversant in the local language. Things seem reversed in this new context whereby Wes' social value is now associated with Grace's instead of the other way around. This is quite unsettling to Wes and he finds himself battling bouts of depression, given he was thrown into an entirely new situation whereby the previous sixty years through which he had come to an understanding of his own social value was made irrelevant overnight. Meanwhile Grace is also contending with a new reality where she is no longer merely someone's wife, but a person in her own right, with her own superior ability to communicate well with the local people. But, having been so used to deferring to Wes in everything, she is lost as to how to grapple with this new situation. The fact that Wes is very unhappy puts a damper on Grace's own sense of thrill in discovering that she is good at adapting to the new culture. In this example, even though Wes and Grace had the finances and the familial support of their children and grandchildren, their challenge in acculturation comes from the process of building social value rather than anything else.

It is important to recognise the role of social value in the process of acculturation, because it plays a significant part in establishing the emotional wellbeing of the migrant. Those who run programs to help new migrants in their process of acculturation would benefit from implementing strategies to help with the migrants' establishment of social value by finding out more about the migrants' life in their former culture and helping them understand how they fit into the social landscape of the new culture.

Often the programs that are designed to assist new migrants focus on helping the migrants understand the new culture without providing the means whereby the migrants' social value in the previous culture is explored. While providing a handbook which explains the rules and expectations of the new culture is helpful, this approach to naturalisation ignores the immigrants' lifetime of experiences prior to migration and does not provide the new immigrant with a pathway to transition from the familiar to the unfamiliar. In other words, many programs for new immigrants present them with a set of schematic structures that are relevant to the host culture. The immigrants are then left with the task of mapping the old schemata to the new ones, in their attempt to understand the cultural context in which they now find themselves. But this task can be daunting, especially if one does not know how to do it. Hence it is often easier for new immigrants to look for others who share their cultural values and remain in diasporas without necessarily attempting to engage with the ways of the host culture. If, however, educating people about perceptual processes and the ways of identifying patterns of familiarity are included as part of training for new immigrants, then they may at least have a pathway to follow, should they choose to engage the ways of the new culture.

Going back to the example of Wes and Grace, Wes' age and gender may no longer automatically give him social value in the new culture, but perhaps if he got connected with other retired accountants or others who share similar interests with him, he may realise that there are different aspects of his life that still hold social value in the new cultural context. Members of the host culture are best poised to assist new immigrants with this process of finding social value because they, as host cultural members, are most familiar with the social currency of the culture. It is akin to a trader from a culture in which the trading currency is chocolates going to another culture in which the trading currency is caramel. At face value, the trader would assume that he has nothing with which to trade in the new culture because his currency is worthless. But a member of the new culture might recognise that the trader has some chocolates that have caramel swirls in them and inform the trader that he can indeed continue to trade in the new culture with those particular caramel-swirl chocolates. In other words, a new immigrant might not readily recognise what s/he can offer to the host culture, but a member of the host culture, by getting to know the immigrant, would be able to recognise the particular skills/abilities of the new immigrant that may meet specific needs in the host culture.

Conversation Break with Chris and Anusha

Anusha: Why do you look so down?

Chris: I just had a conversation with Tom, and it's got me thinking.

Anusha: Who's Tom?

Chris: Tom—you see him every day! He is the janitor who cleans the third floor.

Anusha: Oh, right. I know him by sight, but didn't know his name. So what did you talk about?

Chris: Did you know he has two Masters degrees? And his wife has a MBA. But because neither of them have permanent residency they cannot find a job in their field, so he is working as a janitor and she is a dishwasher at that Thai place down the street.

Anusha: Really? But surely if they are that qualified they can get a job, can't they? I mean companies sponsor permanent residency for employees all the time.

Chris: Yes, but both of them are over forty five, which means it puts them at a disadvantage. When companies hire from overseas, they want younger employees. The older ones with more experience cost much more money and unless you're really a superstar it is hard to get hired at that level.

Anusha: Why did they migrate here then? Couldn't they have stayed with their old jobs in their country?

Chris: They have three kids. And they wanted to get away from the political unrest in their country so that the kids can have a better future. So they're just roughing it out at the moment, doing whatever jobs they can find. It feels so wrong! If I had two Masters degrees I would have a hard time cleaning toilets for a living and feeling like an invisible person that nobody sees. It's like the moment Tom and his wife migrated their social value diminished.

Anusha: Yeah, that must be tough. I would be quite depressed if suddenly I had to go somewhere and had to vacuum the offices of people who are less qualified than I am and people look at me like I'm a nobody. Actually I feel a bit ashamed because I haven't really paid any notice of Tom—I didn't even know his name till just now.

Chris: Well, to be honest we all behave that way from time to time. The point is, I keep thinking it's not right. It's not right that a family had to go to a different country to keep their kids safe but at a great cost to their social value. I don't know what to do about it . . . yet. But I am sure going to find out.

* * *

The Impact of Migration on the Host Society

Though much of early research in acculturation was focused on the psychological and emotional processes of the migrant, recent research, as Berry's (2005) work illustrates, recognises the transformation that migration patterns perpetuate in the host culture as well. Despite the positive associations with multiculturalism in today's society, Liu (2007) for example, found in a study with Asian immigrants and local Australians in Brisbane that while the immigrants in general viewed multiculturalism positively, the locals viewed it as a threat. Liu reasons that multiculturalism is often seen as benefiting the minority groups as opposed to the majority and makes the argument that policy-makers should consider implementing strategies to build confidence in people's cultural identities including that of the majority group, thereby lessening prejudiced attitudes caused by insecurity. This line of reasoning is based on the *Multiculturalism Hypothesis* (Berry et al., 1977) which proposes that feeling secure in one's cultural identity predisposes a person to be more accepting of ethnically different others.

Another hypothesis that is prevalent in acculturation literature is the *Contact Hypothesis* (Allport, 1954; Amir, 1969) which suggests that increased contact between different cultural or ethnic groups will lead to mutual acceptance and lower levels of prejudice. Given certain conditions (such as perceived equality of power, for example), there is evidence to generally support the contact hypothesis (Berry, 2006; Pettigrew & Tropp, 2000). In general, the attitudes of members of the host culture toward immigrants are mixed at best. According to Dunn (2003) 45% of Australians believe that ethnic diversity weakens Australia, while Ward and Masgoret (2006) report that 81% of New Zealanders feel immigrants have something valuable to offer to the country. While 50% of Canadians agree that the number of immigrants in their country is just right, 16% believe that the immigrants pose a threat to the locals' job attainability (Heibert, 2003).

One of the theoretical models which attempts to explain the attitudes of the members of the host culture toward migrants, is the *Integrated Threat Model* (Stephan & Stephan, 2000). The authors identify four types of threats that can be perceived from migrants. First, realistic threats, which are perceived threats to the welfare of the host groups (Ex: competition for limited resources). Second, there are symbolic threats, which are perceived threats to one's culture or way of life. Third, threats caused by inter-group anxiety, and fourth, perception of threat caused by negative stereotypes. Stephan et al. (2005) found that attitudes toward immigrants were most negative in conditions where realistic and symbolic threats are presented together, when members of the host culture perceive the immigrants to be having negative traits, and, that high levels of inter-group anxiety leads to negative attitude towards the migrants. The authors further discovered that differences in beliefs lead to more prejudice than differences in race. This is a significant finding, especially given our tendency to associate inter-group prejudice predominantly with race.

In another study, Stephan and colleagues (1998; 1999) found that anxiety and negative stereotypes were stronger predictors of prejudice toward immigrants than symbolic or realistic threats. This too is an important finding because, given our nature to generalize information in order to simplify the process of understanding (as discussed in Chapter 1), it can be assumed that stereotypes of people groups are prevalent in all societies. These stereotypes are used both humorously as well as in malice. But regardless of intent, stereotypes about people groups do influence societal thinking and may even have adverse effects (Stephan et al., 1998). Lee and Fiske (2006) claim that, "the prevailing stereotype of an immigrant is an incompetent and untrustworthy stranger" (p. 751). Finding from research which correlates negative stereotypes with prejudice toward immigrants is therefore sobering.

According to Berry (2006) greater acceptance of immigrants is situated in the host cultural members' sense of economic and cultural security, as well as *Multicultural Ideology* which he defines as the "general and fundamental view that cultural diversity is good for a society and for its individual members . . . and that diversity should be shared and accommodated in an equitable way" (p. 728). Multicultural ideology in turn is fostered under conditions of low *Social Dominance Orientation* and positive attitudes toward cultural diversity (Ward & Masgoret, 2006). Esses and colleagues (2001) explain Social Dominance Orientation in the following manner:

> Social Dominance Theory assumes that people who are strongly identified with high-status groups and who see intergroup relations in terms of group competition will be especially prejudiced and discriminatory toward outgroups. Individuals high on a measure of individual differences in Social Dominance Orientation believe that unequal social outcomes and social hierarchies are appropriate and therefore support an unequal distribution of resources among groups, often in ways that benefit their own group (p. 398).

The authors go on to explain that perceived group competition fosters negative attitudes toward immigrants. In other words, where members of the host culture see the immigrants as competitors for jobs and resources, there are negative attitudes toward the immigrants, and, according to research findings, those who are high in Social Dominance Orientation view the world as a place in which people groups compete for resources.

Building on previous research in the area of host cultural members' attitudes toward immigrants, Ward and Masgoret (2006) propose an *Integrative Model of Attitude Toward Immigrants* which identifies the variables that contribute to the attitudes that the members of a host culture have toward immigrants. A simplified version of this model is presented here.

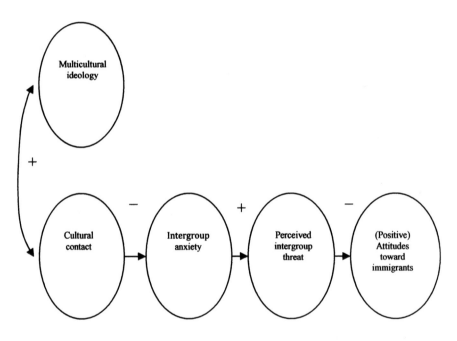

Figure: Integrative model of attitude toward immigrants (Adapted from Ward & Masgoret, 2006)

As the model shows, there is a negative relationship between intercultural contact and intergroup anxiety in the presence of Multicultural Ideology. Further, as intergroup anxiety increases so does perceived intergroup threat (which includes symbolic as well as realistic threats), leading to negative attitudes toward immigrants.

Drawing from a current example in the Australian context, one of the key issues in the 2010 federal elections in Australia was policy regarding "boat people." Driven by the conditions of war in Afghanistan and Sri Lanka, boatloads of asylum-seekers from these countries have been causing headline news in Australia (Allard, 2010; Narushima, 2010). One of the main sentiments expressed in television shows and news debates is the concern as to how the political leaders can prevent boat people from arriving on Australian shores. Though the concern is couched as a concern for the well-being of the people and an attempt to prevent people-smuggling, the underlying fear of border protection is hard to overlook. Despite the fact that the people who arrive by plane and over stay their visa far outnumber asylum seekers who arrive by boat, and despite the fact that the overall number of refugees and migrants represents a miniscule proportion of the Australian population (Corr, 2010), the issue of boat people has commandeered the attention of politicians and voters alike.

This example is illustrative of a larger issue. This is not an issue that is limited to the Australian context. Countries that attract political asylum seekers amass are regularly faced with such issues. When a label such as "boat people" is used to describe a category of people who seek political asylum in another country, it not only generalises them into one faceless mass, but also arguably de-humanises them. Their individual identities are lost behind the generic label. The label characterises them as an outgroup—and as such they are subjected to the perceptual biases that come with ingroup-outgroup interactions (as discussed in Chapter 1). We revert to stereotypical generalisations about the group behind the label, without much consideration of whether the stereotypes apply to all members of that group.

Notwithstanding concerns of "cultural pollution" and xenophobic tendencies, often asylum-seekers are seen as people who come to be an imposition on a country's economy. In a conversation about asylum-seekers, a friend of mine recently observed, "Why shouldn't we welcome asylum-seekers? These are people who have survived wars and political persecution and have exhibited the tenacity and courage needed to survive a perilous boat trip to an unknown land. I think they would make great citizens!" A person who is able to look beyond stereotypical labels and objectively think through the relevant issues is able to see outgroup members with a different perspective. The use of generic labels to describe immigrant groups, however, does not lend itself to such thought processes unless an individual is motivated to look beyond generalisations.

As illustrated in the example of the "boat people," the impact of migration on the host society ranges from the individual level to the political level, even to the point of playing a key role in determining political leadership.

Due to the relevance of immigration patterns and cultural diversification of society in today's industrialised nations, there is proliferation of research on matters of multiculturalism, globalisation, immigrant acculturation, and the effects of cultural diversity on the larger society. A mere glimpse of this research is provided in this chapter. Regardless of whether one belongs to the population of migrants or is a member of a host culture, understanding migration, acculturation, and the implications of cultural diversity is essential to fully understand intercultural communication processes.

Conversation Break with Chris and Anusha

Having been assigned a project called, "Whose Responsibility is it?" for class, Chris and Anusha sit down to discuss the project which requires them to address the effects of immigration on the host society.

Anusha: This is a hard topic. It's so easy to say the wrong thing and be seen as either a prejudiced person or an unpatriotic person! There are just so many complex angles to consider.

Chris: Yes, but that's why it's such an important project for us to do. Let's just say what we think and then we can try to put it all together in some sort of cohesive form for our report.

Anusha: I'm still not clear on the assignment. Are we supposed to answer the question of who is responsible for immigrants?

Chris: Sort of. I think Dr. Walls wants us to think about the different reactions people have to immigrants, the reasons why immigrants may have migrated to our country, the effects of migrants on the social dynamics of the country, that kind of thing.

Anusha: Why don't we start with the social dynamics? I think it's kind of hard when people from different cultures come to an existing culture—it's hard for everyone. For the people in the existing culture, it's like a dimension has been added to their culture and they have to know about it and understand it somehow. As for the migrants, they have to learn the ways of the new culture and try to figure out how they can fit in. I know that they have citizenship classes and things like that to help people understand the new culture, but I still think it's hard. . . . So should the people in the existing culture try to be welcoming and help the new people adapt or should the new people try harder to adapt to the existing culture?

Chris: I think that's one of the key questions we have to think about. But I also think the question is more complex than that. Like Dr. Walls was saying in class, apart from the indigenous people, most of the people in modern-day countries are immigrants—it's a matter of some having been there longer than others. Cultures are continually evolving. So where can we draw the line between who is the new comer and who is part of the existing culture?

Anusha: Good question. It looks like it's going to be a long evening. I better order pizza!

* * *

Intercultural Communication in Multicultural Communities

There are a variety of variables at play when people move from one cultural context to another, as the previous discussion demonstrates. One of the challenges for a migrant, as well as for a person who lives in a community in which there are migrants from other cultures, is to navigate the complexities of intercultural communication in everyday interactions. On the one hand, an argument can be made that a multicultural society is such that every person is entitled to practice his/her own cultural norms. On the other hand, an opposing argument can be made that the migrant has to, at least to an extent, adapt to the expectations of the "mainstream" culture of the host country because the migrant is the new comer into an existing structure. Both of these perspectives are common in culturally diverse societies where people are trying to navigate their own identity as well as where they fit in relation to others. In order to understand the intercultural communication dynamics that unfold in these situations, it is fruitful to take a closer look at a specific instance and unpack it in light of our understanding of intercultural processes. In a study involving the Muslim population in Southern Sydney, Bloch and Dreher (2009) report the following conversation between a couple of elderly white Australian participants and one of the researchers:

S4: We are the aliens. You might think that's strange, but you go for a walk through the park on a Sunday and you'll get looked at and if you say "hello" to anyone—no response.

Int: When you say "they won't meet us halfway," can you say a bit more about that? What would you want them to do?

S5, responding: Just be a bit more friendly! [. . .] When you smile at them and say hello, surely to goodness it's not going to break their little hearts to smile at us and say, "Hello, how are you going, nice day!" That's all! And just appear—even if they can't be bothered being friendly, just appear to be friendly! (p. 203)

As the excerpt reveals, the members of the host culture are expressing the view that they feel alien in their own community due to the arrival of the outsiders who have in essence "taken over" the local space. Due to the large numbers of a particular group of immigrants in that space, the cultural tenor has suddenly shifted such that the dominant norms are those of the immigrants and not of the host culture. Hence a member of the host culture is expressing that, without having chosen to do so, he/she is experiencing being in a "foreign" culture. Based on the comment of the interviewer, it is apparent that the participants who are members of the host culture had expressed that they would like the immigrants to meet them half way in their attempt at intercultural communication. However, based on the response of one of the participants, apparently the immigrants have not done so—thus eliciting further frustration from the host cultural group.

Looking at the situation from the perspective of the immigrants (and here we can only extrapolate what the immigrants' perspective might be, based on our understanding of intercultural communication), one can argue that pockets of diasporas develop because immigrants find comfort in a measure of familiarity in a new place where everything is "alien." Once developed, an immigrant community can function as a "little China" or "little Lebanon" in the midst of New York City or Sydney or wherever the community happens to be, exhibiting the dominant norms of that particular immigrant culture.

Going back to the excerpt from Bloch and Dreher's research, the argument can be made that this particular group of immigrants did not exhibit what the members of the host culture considered to be "friendly" behaviour because the norms of friendliness in their own culture were possibly different from those in the host culture. It is not uncommon in many cultures to reserve smiles or exchanges of pleasantries only for friends and acquaintances. In such cultures it is entirely appropriate for strangers to pass one another on the street without making eye contact or without exchanging a smile. This is not considered unfriendly behaviour but merely "normal" behaviour. Further, immigrants who have not yet mastered the language of the host culture may be reluctant to engage in conversation (even cursory conversation) with someone from the host culture for fear of not understanding or not being understood. Therefore, in order to save face, such an immigrant might avoid conversation all together, even if a member of the host culture initiates it. Regardless of whether it is the appropriate way to behave or not, looking closely at the reasons behind why an immigrant might behave in this way helps one to identify reasons other than racism or intentional rudeness that may be motivating this behaviour.

By the same token the argument can be made that the members of the host culture are entitled to expect others who share their community space to exhibit the norms of polite behaviour as they (the host culture) understand it. They can make the argument that, unlike the immigrants who have arguably *chosen* to live in a different culture, they (the members of the host culture) have not chosen to live in another culture—yet they feel as though they are, because of the large number of immigrants who have influenced the social norms of a particular community.

Switching back to the immigrants' perspective, some immigrants do choose to seclude themselves from the ways of the host culture, thereby attempting to recreate an image of the home culture in their new country, wishing to continue the lifestyle with which they were familiar despite the change in cultural context. This attitude can be equally damaging to intercultural communication just as attitudes of prejudice from members of the host culture can be, because by secluding themselves the immigrants are not only withholding their influence and friendship from members of the host culture but also inadvertently sending a message that though they (the immigrants) need to occupy the land of the host culture, they find the customs of the host culture unworthy of their consumption. Given how closely our identity is connected to our culture, this message, regardless of whether it is sent intentionally or not, can be taken as an offensive one by members of the host culture.

This is everyday reality in many communities today, particularly in countries like the United States, Australia, New Zealand, and the United Kingdom where populations of immigrants have settled over the past few decades. An interesting fact to note is that the extent to which a member of the host culture can lay prior claim to the country is questionable in several of these countries which are in turn made up of immigrants who are not indigenous to the land. The point is, much miscommunication and strife are propagated based on our perception of the objectivity of some concepts (such as nationality) that are arbitrary to begin with. That is, in nations that are predominantly made up of immigrants, how far back in history does one have to go in order to be considered a "true" native of the land? Referring back to the discussion in Chapter 2 about the arbitrary nature of concepts such as nationality, citizenship, and ingroups, it is prudent that we are mindful, when engaging cultural diversity in our community, not to base our decisions on reified human structures which are in fact negotiable.

Chapter Five
INTERCULTURAL COMMUNICATION COMPETENCE

I recall sitting in a graduate seminar one day, listening to the professor speak about the use of technology in communication. What made that otherwise indistinct day memorable was that the professor made (what I perceived as) an uninformed remark about developing countries. It was the way in which the remark was made that made me notice it—the professor said something about how someone in a remote corner of the world might be sitting with a small antenna, trying to download files from the Internet. But the place he named as an example of such a remote part of the world happened to be a place where I had been, and a place where high-speed Internet services were readily accessible in a variety of forms. I remember thinking at that moment that this professor probably had never been to that place—because if he had, then he would've known that the place he perceived to be "some remote corner" in a developing country was in fact a thriving modern-day metropolis. Yet he confidently used that place as an example of a remote location based on his perception of it, possibly from hearing its name somewhere. The manner in which he spoke of this "remote corner" of the world was dismissive, and that is what stood out to me that day. It was a passing remark, yet it made an impression on me because it made me think about the notion of communication competence. Even though he was a professor of communication, his uninformed remark made him lose credibility in my eyes, especially as an international student who was very much attuned to cultural perceptions.

Around the same time as I made this observation, I experienced another incident that made me think deeper about intercultural communication competence. As part of a community outreach program organised by the university, a few international students (including myself) were asked to visit a school in a rural town in Kentucky, to share our experiences and tell the children about our various cultures. We had the opportunity to interact with people who had never met a person from a different culture or even seen someone who wasn't white. Yet I noticed that some of the people in this town communicated with a measure of warmth and perceptiveness that I found inviting. Though they had no training in intercultural communication and no prior experience in interacting with people from other cultures, they were still able to communicate effectively and appropriately. Their astuteness and unassuming manner somehow stood in contrast to that of the professor in my class.

As a student of communication, I began to think about what enabled those people in rural Kentucky to be perceived as competent intercultural communicators when someone who is trained in communication, like the professor in the seminar, could not manage it. Little did I know that these events would inspire what turned out to be my doctoral dissertation and the research in intercultural communication competence (ICC) I've pursued since then.

The desire to be competent in intercultural communication is strong in those of us who operate in today's culturally diverse societies in which the difference between an effective cultural exchange and an intercultural blunder could potentially cost millions of dollars, let alone the goodwill of a potential friend, colleague, or client. But what exactly does it mean for us to communicate competently with someone from a different culture? Further, who qualifies as someone from a *different* culture? Are there key "ingredients" or variables which contribute to competent intercultural communication regardless of context? These are questions worth exploring. In order to progress forward in the process of invention, often one has to look behind to take stock of what has already been accomplished. A comprehensive review of previous models of intercultural communication competence is beyond the scope of this chapter (see Spitzberg & Chagnon, 2009, for such a review). I would, however, like to briefly highlight some key thoughts in ICC research.

Spitzberg and Cupach (1984) describe communication competence in terms of *effective* and *appropriate* behaviour. A communication exchange is effective if one is able to accomplish one's goal for that particular exchange, and appropriate if s/he is able to do so while exhibiting behaviour that is both expected and accepted in the given social context. Needless to say, cultural idiosyncrasies dictate what is considered effective and appropriate. The study of competent intercultural communication therefore presents an added dimension of complexity.

Theoretical Approaches to ICC

A survey of literature in intercultural communication reveals that there is need for clarification of some of the terms that are used most frequently in intercultural communication research. For example, there is vast literature in adaptation/acculturation processes (Kim, 1995, 2001; Kim & Ruben, 1988; Ruben, 1983), identity and face negotiation (Ting-Toomey, 1993), and uncertainty and anxiety management (Gudykunst, 1993, 1995). However, there seems to be some overlap in the use of certain terms that describe different concepts. It is helpful at this point to define what the researchers mean by each one of these terms in order to clarify exactly what is being studied.

One of the most widely used theories in intercultural communication is the Anxiety/Uncertainty Management theory (AUM) by Gudykunst (Gudykunst, 1993, 1995; Stephan, Stephan, & Gudykunst, 1999). The AUM theory is based on the premise that a basic cause for effective communication between "strangers" (people who do not belong to the same in-group) is anxiety and uncertainty management. Gudykunst (1993) extends Berger and Calabrese's (1975) uncertainty reduction theory to intercultural communication and argues that because intercultural encounters are novel situations, this means that there are high levels of anxiety and uncertainty associated with them. He further argues that a person's effective communication with strangers is influenced by his/her ability to be mindful of their own behaviour because being mindful regulates anxiety/uncertainty management. In this approach, "effective communication refers to minimising misunderstanding" (Gudykunst, 1993, p. 34).

Despite the fact that AUM theory is widely researched (Gudykunst & Nishida, 2001; Stephan, Stephan, & Gudykunst, 1999), it is not without its critics. Yoshitake (2002), for example, points out that the focus of AUM theory is limited to effective communication. Effective communication in the context of AUM theory refers to communication with the least possible misunderstanding. Yoshitake argues that there are instances where attributing the closest meaning to a message is not only impossible but also unnecessary. This argument is based on the reasoning that reducing effective communication to minimising misunderstanding implies a linear view of communication (consisting of a sender, message, and a receiver) that is not necessarily representative of reality. Yoshitake also points out that by relying on mindfulness as a key element of uncertainty/anxiety management, AUM theory heavily relies on consciousness. This does not account for situations where emotional decisions (that are not necessarily rational) are made. The third criticism of the theory is that AUM theory has a Western bias. Yoshitake argues that AUM theory reflects cultural values that are typical of America and that these values are imposed on other cultures by extending the theory to intercultural situations.

Another theoretical approach used frequently in ICC literature is identity negotiation (Ting-Toomey, 1993). Ting-Toomey defines ICC as "the effective identity negotiation process between two or more interactants in a novel communication episode" (p. 73). Novelty, in turn, is characterised as a situation that contains "both unpredictability and challenge" (p. 73), and identity is defined as, "the mosaic sense of self-identification that incorporates the interplay of human, cultural, social, and personal images as consciously or unconsciously experienced and enacted by the individual" (p. 74). The identity negotiation model provides a valuable framework for understanding the internal processes that the "self" experiences in an intercultural situation.

To name another theoretical approach, Spitzberg (1997) proposes what he calls an integrative model of ICC that represents three levels of analysis: 1) the individual system (the individual's characteristics that contribute to competence in interactions), 2) the episodic system (factors that contribute to perceived competence in a particular interaction/context), and 3) the relational system (the characteristics of an individual that contribute to competence in relationships in general). Motivation (to communicate competently), knowledge (of how to communicate competently), and skills (behavioural enactment of knowledge) are identified as components of the individual system. Spitzberg claims that as each of these components increase, so does competence in communication.

Knowledge, attitude, and skills appear as recurring themes in research in ICC. Deardorff (2006; 2009), for example, identifies specific variables associated with each of these three larger categories, in her *Process Model of Intercultural Competence*. The model identifies the attitudes of respect, openness and curiosity as baseline prerequisites upon which the knowledge elements of cultural self-awareness, culture-specific information, and sociolinguistic awareness as well as the skills of listening, observing, interpreting, analysing, evaluating and relating, rest. The model also identified desired internal and external outcomes in the context of intercultural competence.

Though these models by no means represent an exhaustive list of models of ICC, they are representative of some of the popular models in intercultural communication literature. Presenting the argument that there is need for a model of intercultural communication competence that incorporates multiple cultural perspectives, Arasaratnam and Doerfel (2005) published a study in which qualitative data were collected from participants who represented fifteen countries. The basic premise of the study was to address the question, "What, if any, are variables which contribute to ICC across cultures?"

Each participant was asked to describe a competent intercultural communicator and the characteristics s/he sees in such a person. If commonalities exist in the way people from different cultures perceive competent intercultural communication, then those would have arisen in these descriptions by the participants who represented fifteen cultural perspectives. Using semantic network analysis, which enables the researcher to extract dominant themes in textual data, the authors looked for themes in the responses of the participants.

Five variables emerged as dominant themes namely; empathy, experience/training in interacting with people of other cultures, positive attitude toward people of other cultures, ability to listen effectively, and motivation to communicate with people from other cultures. Having identified these variables, it was time to build a model of ICC.

The Integrated Model of Intercultural Communication Competence

The *Integrated Model of Intercultural Communication Competence* (IMICC) identifies five key variables which contribute to behaviour that is perceived as competent intercultural communication (Arasaratnam, 2006; Arasaratnam & Banerjee, 2007; Arasaratnam, Banerjee, & Dembek, 2010a). The IMICC is a causal model, depicting the relationship between these five variables and how they contribute to ICC. One of the unique factors of the IMICC is its inductive design incorporating how intercultural communication is perceived from different cultural perspectives.

The model identifies empathy and experience as exogenous variables that, in interaction with motivation, listening, and positive attitude towards other cultures, contribute to ICC. According to the IMICC, experience/training in intercultural communication leads to positive attitudes toward people of other cultures which leads to motivation to engage in intercultural communication which in turn leads to more experience in intercultural communication. This cycle also feeds into a person's ICC. The model also proposes that an empathetic person is one who is able to be an engaged listener, thereby being perceived as a competent intercultural communicator. Motivation to communicate with people from other cultures also leads to active listening when communicating with someone from a different culture, which in turn leads to the perception of ICC from the other person. Because the model is based on the results of Arasaratnam and Doerfel's (2005) study in which ICC was described from the perspective of the *perceiver*, the ICC variable in IMICC is in fact *perceived* ICC, from the perspective of the culturally different other. In other words, IMICC proposes that the five key variables identified in the model contribute to a person being perceived as a competent intercultural communicator. This is an important point to note, as researchers have been calling for ICC to be studied from the perspective of the perceiver for some time (Collier, 1989).

The model does not account for differences in languages in intercultural interactions; it does, however, provide an explanation as to how someone who has no training in or exposure to intercultural communication can still be perceived as a competent intercultural communicator. This thought will be explored in further detail later. First, it is helpful to discuss each of the variables identified in IMICC.

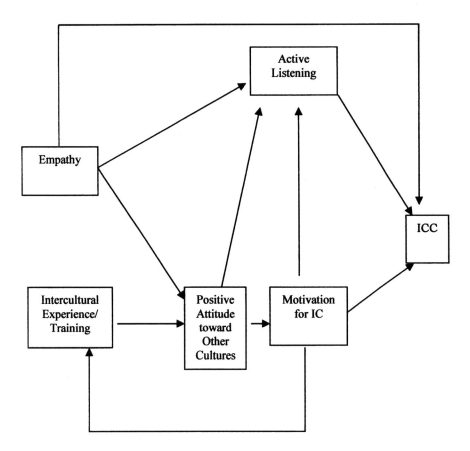

Figure: The Integrated Model of Intercultural Communication Competence (adapted from Arasaratnam, 2006; Arasaratnam, Banerjee, & Dembek, 2010a).

Empathy

Empathy is commonly understood as the ability to engage in cognitive and emotional or affective role-playing (Docety & Jackson, 2004), with the outcome of a deeper understanding of and appreciation for another person's experiences. Knafo et al. (2008) explain

> The cognitive aspect of empathy entails an ability to effectively comprehend a distressing situation and to recognise another's emotions and assume that person's perspective. . . . The affective aspect of empathy requires an individual to experience a vicarious emotional response to others' expressed emotions (p. 737).

A person who has the ability to empathise may not necessarily have experienced something similar to the other person, but has the capability to not only imagine how such an experience could feel but also vicariously engage the emotions that the other person may be experiencing. Knafo et al. also note that empathy is a disposition that is stable across developmental stages as well as contexts. De Wall (2008) identifies three levels of empathy: 1) *Emotional contagion*—this is where a person is affected by another person's emotional arousal or emotional state 2) *Sympathetic concern*—in addition to being affected by the other person's emotional condition, at this level of empathy a person tries to evaluate the situation and understand the reason for the other person's emotional condition 3) *Empathic perspective-taking*—at this level the person not only engages with the other person's emotions but also takes on the other's point of view using one's imagination. De Wall argues that people who are highly self-aware are able to empathise at the third level effectively while keeping things in perspective, without losing sight of the fact they are experiencing someone else's emotions.

In the context of intercultural communication, a variable that is often discussed is cultural empathy. Ruben (1976) defines it as, "the capacity to clearly project an interest in others, as well as to obtain and to reflect a reasonably complete and accurate sense of another's thoughts, feelings, and/or experiences" (p. 340). Cultural empathy is one of the key variables featured in the widely used *Multicultural Personality Questionnaire* (Van der Zee & Van Oudenhoven, 2000).

There is a vast body of literature on empathy. For the purposes of the current discussion, it is helpful to understand why an empathetic person would be perceived as a competent intercultural communicator. Research reveals that empathy triggers altruism such that, "under conditions of high empathy people want to help the other at a considerable cost to self even if they could simply leave the situation in an effort to reduce their own distress" (Van Lange, 2008, p. 767). This is arguably a desirable quality in a communicator because often intercultural communication occurs in situations where one or both persons are in need of help—at the very least, help with understanding the other. Empathy presents a possible explanation as to how a person who isn't an experienced intercultural communicator may still be perceived as a competent intercultural communicator (as in the case of the people whom I met in rural Kentucky). Though a person might not have had the opportunity travel or interact with people from other cultures, the Integrated Model of ICC suggests that if that person is empathetic, then he/she could still exhibit competence in intercultural communication.

Listening

The ability to be an active listener is another variable that is associated with ICC. Active listening is a genuine attempt to receive what the other person is communicating without bias or predetermined agenda. Regardless of cultural context, the ability to listen effectively is arguably a virtue when it comes to communication competence. The specific behaviours that are perceived to be active listening, however, need further exploration. In a study to determine the significance of paraphrasing as a form of active listening, Weger, Castle and Emmett (2010) discovered that though paraphrasing enables the listener to be perceived as likable, it did not make the participants feel understood or satisfied with the conversation. The authors posit that perhaps people are more attuned to the nonverbal cues of listeners rather than the verbal act of paraphrasing. The participants in Arasaratnam and Doerfel's study also indicated that nonverbal cues such as nodding, eye contact, displaying appropriate facial expressions, are important in determining whether someone is listening.

Research also reveals that those who are oriented or attuned to others are also high self-monitors. Cheng and Chartrand (2003), for example, found that high self-minors non-consciously mimicked the nonverbal behaviour of people whom they perceived as their peers, as a means of affiliation. The researchers argue that this is due to the fact that high self-minors are attuned to environmental cues in such a way that they mimic behaviours as a way of relating to the other person without consciously processing what they are doing. This is an important finding because, as mentioned in a previous chapter, there are cultural differences in nonverbal etiquette; and so the act of exhibiting appropriate nonverbal cues as indicators of active listening can be challenging in intercultural spaces. However, as Cheng and Chartrand's study reveals, a high self-monitor is able to mimic the other person's nonverbal cues in a subtle and non-conscious way whereby creating a sense of camaraderie and affiliation. This, in combination with the evidence which suggests that mimickers are more liked than non-mimickers (Lakin & Chartrand, 2003), provides a glimpse of one aspect of the dynamics of active listening.

Experience/Training

This variable encompasses prior exposure to intercultural situations (international travel, interaction with people from other cultures, etc.) as well as training and/or education in intercultural communication. Arguably, a person who has prior experience in communicating with people from other cultures has more practice in doing so and is better equipped to do so than someone who has no prior experience. This argument is based on the assumption that experience and training leads to knowledge, which in turn can be utilised appropriately in behaviour. There are, however, certain caveats that must be noted.

McAllister and colleagues (2006) argue that intercultural learning through exposure to people of other cultures or experience travelling to other cultures happens through personal reflection and critical thinking. In other words, just because someone has vast experience travelling to many countries, it does not necessarily mean that s/he will automatically develop intercultural competence. There is an element of personal reflection that is involved in learning from one's experiences. Further, a similar observation can be made about intercultural training or education—mere exposure to training does not necessarily lead to increased competence. As in any other learning process, there is a measure of reflection and internalization that needs to occur in order for training and education to be translated into practical application. Even if acquisition of knowledge has occurred through learning and intercultural experiences, a person might still choose not to act on that knowledge based on personal convictions or preferences. For example, in a study of postgraduate international students in America, Arasaratnam (2003) discovered that in some instances, though the international students had the knowledge and the skill to adopt the dominant style of communication in graduate seminars, they chose not to do so because the assertive style of communication did not appeal to them.

There is evidence to suggest, however, that intercultural experiences and training shape attitudes because attitudes are most accessible when there is direct experience with the phenomenon in question, repeated exposure to the particular attitude in question, and opportunity to reflect on the attitude (Robinovich, Morten, & Postmes, 2010). Attitudes, in turn, play an important role in perception of intercultural communication competence, according to the participants in Arasaratnam and Doerfel's (2005) study.

Positive Attitude toward Other Cultures

This variable refers to a predisposition toward favourably evaluating people of other cultures, based on a non-ethnocentric view of the world. van der Zee and van Oudenhoven (2000) refer to a similar variable in the Multicultural Personality Questionnaire (MPQ), which they name "open mindedness." A person who has an attitude that people from other cultures merely represent alternative perspectives of the world (as opposed to presenting a threat to one's own worldview) is predisposed to favourably engaging in intercultural communication and therefore being perceived favourably by the other party. This was evident from Arasaratnam and Doerfel's (2005) findings.

There is an intimate connection between knowledge, attitude, and behaviour. Fabrigar and colleagues (2006) identify two characteristics of attitude-relevant knowledge that guide behaviour. First, is the "degree to which the content of the knowledge on which the attitude is based is directly relevant to the goal of the behaviour" (p. 558). Second, is "the complexity of the knowledge underlying the attitude" (p. 558). The more complex the dimensions of knowledge, the more one can expect attitude to influence behaviour. For example, people who have differentiated and complex knowledge about a particular cultural group (perhaps from person experiences, formal study, critical reflection, etc.) are less likely to be influenced by ambiguous or a particular anomalous behaviour by a member of that cultural group than people whose knowledge of that group is undifferentiated and simplistic. Fabrigar and colleagues explain:

> For instance, when a person has an attitude based on a single dimension of knowledge and that dimension has little direct relevance to the goal of the behaviour, a person might conclude that the attitude is not a very informative guide . . . However, if the attitude is based on multiple distinct dimensions of knowledge that are evaluatively consistent with one another, a person might assume that other potential dimensions of knowledge for which the person has no information are likely to be evaluatively similar to the dimensions from which the attitude is derived. That is, the person might be willing to extrapolate to and make inferences about dimensions of attitude-relevant information for which the person has no current knowledge (pp. 558-559).

It is important to understand that mere acquisition of knowledge doesn't lead to change in attitudes, and the possession of certain attitudes does not always translate into behaviour that is consistent with those attitudes. This understanding is particularly relevant in the context of intercultural communication because it would be simplistic for one to say that positive attitude towards other cultures always leads to positive or friendly behaviour toward people from other cultures.

Another important distinction to be considered when discussing attitudes toward people of other cultures is between the cognition and the affect associated with that attitude. In this instance, *cognition* refers to knowledge-based beliefs (both positive and negative) about the attitude toward other cultures and *affect* refers to the feelings or emotions (again, both positive and negative) about the attitude toward other cultures. For example, Jim might have negative attitude toward other cultures because he feels threatened (affect) by people who are different based on hearing news stories that immigrants are taking over jobs from members of the host community (cognition). Depending on the extent to which the person's attitude is reliant on an affective or cognitive structural base, the person is susceptible to be persuaded to change his/her attitude if the persuasive message targets the appropriate base (See, Petty, & Fabrigar, 2008). In other words, going back to the example of Jim, if Jim's negative attitude toward other cultures is more reliant on a cognitive base, then Jim might be influenced by a persuasive message which says that even though immigrants are indeed competing for jobs with the members of the host community, this process is also stimulating the economy and leading to the creation of more jobs. If Jim's negative attitude is mostly based on affect, then a cognitive appeal is unlikely to persuade him to change his attitude.

Motivation

This variable refers to a person's motivation or drive to engage in intercultural communication. As the model depicts, attitude and motivation are linked such that positive attitude toward other cultures leads to motivation to engage in intercultural communication which in turn leads to more experience in intercultural communication (if the motivation results in the actual behaviour of communicating with people from other cultures). There are many possible reasons for why one may be motivated to engage in intercultural communication, including a reason which possibly has a biological basis. This will be discussed further in the next section on sensation seeking and intercultural communication. Returning our attention to the role of motivation in intercultural communication competence, the participants in Arasaratnam and Doerfel's (2005) study indicated that when someone from another culture seems interested in or keen to talk to them, they perceive that person favourably—they perceive him/her to be a competent intercultural communicator. They described this quality of the communicator as being "motivated" to engage in intercultural communication, and expressed that such motivation facilitates a favourable perception of the communicator (which the participants interpreted as "competence"). Further research reveals that motivation to interact with people from other cultures may contribute to ICC by stimulating exposure to a variety of intercultural exchanges and in turn contributing to positive attitude toward other cultures (Arasaratnam, 2006).

A question that is worth exploring is what would motivate someone to engage in intercultural communication? Perhaps the motivation might arise from a desire to know more about the world and experience new things firsthand. Or one might have empathetic or altruistic motivations to interact with new immigrants or international students with the goal of helping them find their place in the host community. Alternatively, one might be motivated by a drive to survive, if one finds one's self in a new culture and needs to communicate with others to find answers or information. One of the strongest sources of motivation to experience intercultural communication appears to be biological, based on research on the role of sensation seeking in intercultural communication.

Sensation Seeking and Intercultural Communication

One of the key personality variables that has been associated with drug, alcohol and tobacco use, especially in younger users, is sensation seeking. High sensation seekers are known for their thirst for thrill, adventure and novelty, low attention span, and propensity toward risky behaviour (Everett & Palmgreen, 1995; Palmgreen & Donohew; 1994). It is their affinity for novel and exciting experiences that draw high sensation seekers toward activities such as bungee jumping, sky diving, cliff climbing, etc. Research shows that this thirst for adventure and experimentation is also a predisposition toward drug and tobacco use. Drug prevention campaigns which target high sensation seekers have produced successful results (Palmgreen et al., 2001).

Assuming that the same thirst for novelty which predisposes high sensation seekers to try drugs or alcohol may also predispose them toward experiencing intercultural contact (because of the novel element inherent in such experiences), Morgan and Arasaratnam (2003) took the research in sensation seeking in a new direction, making a connection between sensation seeking and intercultural contact. The researchers also reasoned that the affinity that high sensation seekers have for thrilling and risky experiences may extend to experiences of intercultural contact as well because of the social risk involved in such experiences. In other words, just as the risk and "danger" involved in sky diving elicits an adrenaline rush, the risk of engaging the unknown and the potential for losing face or social embarrassment in an intercultural situation may also provide a "rush" for the high sensation seeker. Morgan and Arasaratnam's study revealed that there is indeed a connection between sensation seeking and attributes that are conducive to the formation of intercultural friendships. Following this, further research (Arasaratnam, 2004; Arasaratnam & Banerjee, 2007) revealed that high sensation seekers are more likely to seek intercultural contact and friendships compared to low sensation seekers. In a study involving international students in the United States, Arasaratnam (2005), for example, found that the high sensation seekers amongst the students reported a higher sense of overall satisfaction in their study abroad experience compared to their low sensation seeking counterparts. Arasaratnam also found that there is a direct relationship between sensation seeking and motivation to interact with people from other cultures, and, motivation is directly related to intercultural contact-seeking behaviour which in turn contributes to greater satisfaction of the overall experience of studying abroad.

In an effort to explore whether high sensation seekers are also prone to be perceived as high in ICC, Arasaratnam & Banerjee (2009) conducted a study to test the relationship between sensation seeking and ICC via a theoretical model based on a previous study, also conducted by Arasaratnam and Banerjee (2007). The researchers found that sensation seeking is indeed positively related to ICC. Given high sensation seekers are motivated to look for opportunities for intercultural contact, and given higher experience in intercultural communication leads to higher levels of ICC (according to IMICC) providing a positive attitude toward other cultures, it could be assumed that high sensation seekers will also be high in ICC. The evidence from research, however, does not support any direct relationship between sensation seeking and ICC (Arasaratnam, Banerjee, Dembek, 2010b) so far. It is interesting to note, however, that in the same study in which Arasaratnam, Banerjee and Dembek failed to discover a direct relationship between sensation seeking and ICC, they also discovered that there is a direct relationship between sensation seeking and interaction involvement.

In other words, it appears that high sensation seekers are active/involved listeners when interacting with people from other cultures. Given active listening is one of the key variables in the Integrated Model of ICC, this is yet another indirect connection between sensation seeking and ICC. However, based on the findings so far, it can only be concluded that sensation seeking serves as a motivating factor to engage in intercultural communication, but there is no evidence to suggest a direct relationship between sensation seeking and intercultural communication competence.

The pragmatic implications of the findings in studies of sensation seeking and intercultural communication are yet to be unpacked, as this line of research is still in its early stages. The possibility of encouraging intercultural contact as a socially acceptable alternative to other dangerous ways of thrill-seeking to satiate the appetite of high sensation seekers is yet to be fully explored.

Conversation Break with Chris and Anusha

Chris: Are you going to Brad's party this weekend?

Anusha: No, I can't.

Chris: Why not? I thought you're white water rafting trip isn't till next weekend. What, are you going skydiving this weekend or something?

Anusha: Very funny. Just because I like to do adventurous things, it doesn't mean that's *all* I do. Actually this weekend I'm volunteering at the international student services office. They have an orientation for new international students.

Chris: Really? What do the volunteers do?

Anusha: We just help organise things and answer any questions that the new students may have. I do it pretty much every year. I like meeting people from different countries.

Chris: Do you get training for that sort of thing? I'd be afraid I'd say the wrong thing and insult someone from a different culture.

Anusha: Yeah, I guess that's always a risk, but it's kind of a rush too—not knowing what to expect.

Chris: I guess that's the high sensation seeker in you talking.

Anusha: Oh yes, that's me! Did you take the sensation seeking test in class too? What was your result?

Chris: I came right in the middle—neither high, nor low. Maybe I'll come with you this weekend and see what you do with the international students. I'd like to help out, but it would be good to observe how things are done first.

Anusha: Being cautious, are you? Where's the fun in that? (Grins). OK, you can come along on Saturday. Maybe it will whet your appetite for adventurous experiences!

* * *

Developing Intercultural Communication Competence

The discussions on perceptual processes, social cognition, and various other topics related to intercultural communication in the previous chapters highlight the complexity of the process such that developing intercultural communication competence should not be mistaken for mere skill development. Skills tell us the "what" and the "how," but not necessarily the "why." Hence developing intercultural communication competence is a multi-pronged process of introspection, developing self-awareness, deconstruction of perceptual biases, perspective-taking, and the acquisition of relevant skills.

In her article on cultivating intercultural competence, Bennett (2009) proposes that competence in intercultural communication involves the navigation of both culture-general as well as culture-specific factors. Bennett identifies categories such as nonverbal behaviour, learning styles, communication styles, etc. as culture-general, and categories that are particular to cultures (such as the conversation turn-taking rituals in Ghana, for example) as culture-specific. Further, Bennett argues that one must first locate one's own cultural position in these matters through self-awareness before one can identify how to relate to others who are different.

Change in behaviour begins with change in attitudes, which in turn begins with change in beliefs and values (Ajzen & Fishbein, 1980). Therefore developing a positive attitude toward people of other cultures is a good place to start. The concept of in and outgroups was discussed in Chapter 1. Given ingroups and outgroups are fluid entities and given we are predisposed to perceiving our ingroup members more favourably than outgroup members; it stands to reason that focusing on categories which facilitate the formation of ingroups consisting of people from different cultures is helpful.

Having watched more than the average person's share of sci-fi movies, I've noticed something fascinating: when an alien race threatens humanity, all humans somehow put aside their centuries of wars and hostility and band together to defend earth. Within the group of humans, enemies who once fought viciously against each other willingly find themselves on the same team. In the face of a common enemy, suddenly a new ingroup is formed: humans vs. aliens.

Alien invasion notwithstanding, there are other strategies that can be implemented to create ingroups that are inclusive of persons from a variety of cultural backgrounds. A good example is portrayed in the movie *Freedom Writers* (LaGravenese, 2007). Ms. G, the teacher, urges the class to participate in the "line game" in an effort to bring cohesion in a group of students who were segregated due to bitter hostility between ethnic groups. In the line game, the teacher calls out a category such as, "Stand on the line if you know someone who was killed in gang violence" and then the students to whom that category was applicable would step up to the line while others would back off. Ms. G calls out various categories, forcing students from different ethnic groups to step up to the line together while simultaneously enabling them to realise that someone else of a different * shares a common experience with them. By highlighting categories other than ethnic differences, the line game facilitates the breakdown of previously existing ingroups and outgroups in which ethnicity was the defining category.

The creation of new ingroups that are inclusive of multiple cultures is easier in an organisational setting. If cohesion between members of the organisation is the goal, then the leaders of the organisation can intentionally create a culture that is unique to the organisation and repeatedly use strategic rhetoric to facilitate the formation of a new ingroup to which all members of the organisation belong, regardless of their nationality or ethnic culture. Given there is an extensive body of literature on organisational communication and organisational culture it is unnecessary to belabour the point here. However, to quickly highlight some key strategies, an organisational culture can be intentionally created by collectively coming up with a mission/vision statement, reinforcing the organisation's values (which should also be clearly articulated) in explicit ways, and coming up with rituals or activities in which all members of the organisation participate such that unique organisational traditions are created. Such unification of people from different cultures under one ingroup is already seen in places like churches, community groups and other such organisations where people share certain core values such that the defining variable is no longer cultural affiliation.

As the model illustrates, intercultural experiences also arguably increase awareness and expose one to cultural perspectives other than one's own. But this exposure alone does not necessarily lead to positive attitude toward people of other cultures. As discussed in Chapter 1, a person who is predisposed to maintaining existing (negative) stereotypes might find ways of reinforcing his/her prior beliefs by interpreting intercultural experiences in a way in which they reinforce the stereotypes. Hence, in any study abroad or other program designed to increase cultural awareness and foster positive attitudes toward other cultures, it is essential to first prepare the participants beforehand by addressing their beliefs.

The IMICC identifies listening as a key skill which contributes to perceived ICC. Based on the responses of the participants in Arasaratnam and Doerfel's (2005) study, listening was characterised in terms of one's ability to show the relevant nonverbal signals (such as nodding and engaging in appropriate eye contact) as well as asking inviting follow-up questions. In addition to this everyday observation of what listening entails, it is necessary to view listening in light of one's understanding of varying styles of communication as well. For example, a person who is conversant in low context style of communication may be a good listener to someone who also communicates in that style, but unskilled at listening to a high context communicator either due to lack of practice or due to lack of knowledge and/or skills to recognise and interpret high context cues. As in any other skill, the ability to listen effectively arguably increases with deliberate practice. Practicing listening effectively in high context mode inherently involves understanding the cultural context in which the communicator operates. Further, skilled high context listening develops with longer exposure to high context communicators as well as the relevant cultural context. The ability to discern whether someone is communicating in low or high context mode is also part of the art of listening effectively. Though there are no simplistic, formulaic ways of determining one's mode of communication, an astute listener can observe whether a communicator is being verbally explicit or not by engaging in conversation and asking subtle follow-up questions.

Mini Case Study

Harry: Mandy, if you have time this afternoon, could you please proof read the building project proposal?

Mandy: I'm finishing up the marketing report that needs to go to the sixth floor by 5pm.

Harry: I see. How far along are you?

Mandy: About half-way through. How urgently does the proof reading need to be done?

Harry: Um . . . actually, it too has to go up to sixth by the end of the day. But I can see you're quite busy, so I'll check with Ted whether he can do it.

Questions to Ponder

1. Does Harry or Mandy (or both) engage in high context communication? Justify your view.

2. Does either one of these characters exemplify good listening? If so, why?
3. What have you learned about listening, from this case study?

* * *

Intercultural Scenarios

Gudykunst and Kim (2003) espouse the idea of *mindfulness* in developing and achieving effective intercultural communication, as mentioned in the description of the AUM model previously. A *mindful* communicator is constantly alert to subtle nuances in the communication exchange, thus observing and learning from different intercultural situations. Ideally, intentional exposure to intercultural situations and mindful observation are likely to enhance a person's understanding of intercultural communication. However, for training purposes, often intercultural scenarios are used as a means of highlighting relevant issues (Herfst, van Oudenhoven & Timmerman, 2008).

Despite the artificial nature of staged critical incidents, this process enables one to systematically reflect on intercultural issues in a safe and controlled environment. Critical incidents or scenarios are also effective tools in classroom or training settings which do not always lend themselves to direct experiential learning.

The following scenarios are examples of critical incidents that can be used to assess appropriate behaviour in intercultural communication contexts. Each of the scenarios is followed by four possible courses of action. To experience learning through critical incidents, rank each suggested course of action according to your preference, ranking the most preferred course of action 1 and the least preferred one 4.

Scenario 1

Jane and her friends are invited to dinner by one of their friends who is from a different culture. When they arrived at their friend's apartment, they notice that their friend has prepared food from her culture. As the dishes are passed around the table, Jane realises that she doesn't like the smell of some of the dishes. She doesn't want to offend her host by not eating her cooking, but she doesn't want to get sick at the table either. What should she do?

1) Tell her friend that something came up unexpectedly and leave before the dinner starts.

Rank ___

2) Ask questions about the dishes and how they are prepared.

Rank ___

3) Explain that she doesn't like the smells and politely decline the food.

Rank ___

4) Try a little bit of the food to see what it tastes like.

Rank ___

Scenario 2

Ann and Wei Li are roommates. Ann likes to invite her friends over to her apartment often, and Wei Li finds herself feeling uncomfortable with this situation. It is not customary in Wei Li's culture to be confrontational. So she feels hesitant about voicing her feelings to Ann. How should Wei Li deal with this situation?

1) Wei Li should show her displeasure in indirect ways such as staying in her room while Ann's friends are over.

Rank ___

2) Wei Li should ask someone else from Ann's culture about the best way to approach this situation.

Rank ___

3) Wei Li should ask Ann whether they could schedule times for having visitors over.

Rank ___

4) Wei Li should invite her own friends to come often so Ann would know what it feels like.

Rank ___

Scenario 3

Eric is a visitor in Omi's country. As Omi began to get to know Eric, he realises that many of Eric's ways and attitudes are offensive to people of Omi's culture. Omi doesn't want Eric to have a bad reputation in his culture, but he doesn't know how to let Eric know about this without hurting Eric's feelings. Also, subtlety is valued in Omi's culture. So Omi isn't accustomed to speaking about things openly. How can Omi help Eric?

1) Omi should ask Eric questions about his understanding of Omi's culture, to open a discussion.

Rank ___

2) Every time Eric offends someone, Omi can discreetly explain to that person that Eric is new to the country.

Rank ___

3) Omi can indirectly tell Eric how he is feeling by narrating it like a story about someone else, where the characters will represent Omi and Eric.

Rank ___

4) Omi can start avoiding Eric for a while, to indirectly let him know that he is offensive.

Rank ___

Scenario 4

Tom is part of a group that is assigned to complete a task. The group members decide that everyone will pair up with one other person to work on different aspects of the task. The person that Tom gets paired with is a lady from a different culture. As Tom starts making conversation with this person, he realises that he has a very hard time understanding her accent. Tom tries asking her to repeat herself a couple of times, but he still couldn't understand what she was saying. How should Tom handle this situation?

1) Ask the lady whether she has trouble understanding him.

Rank ___

2) Explain the situation to the group leader and ask for another partner.

Rank ___

3) Suggest to the lady that they should both write down their ideas for each other.

Rank ___

4) Explain to the lady that he wishes to work with someone else because he has trouble understanding her.

Rank ___

Explanation of the Scenarios

Scenario 1

Often food is very personal to people and it can be an intimate expression of a culture or of friendship. Therefore one shouldn't respond with distaste or aversion when someone offers food. The diplomatic way to handle such a situation is to engage the other person in conversation about how the food is prepared, what the significance of the food is, etc., thus showing appreciation for the culture and the effort that has gone into the food preparation. If personal religious or health reasons don't prohibit, it is also preferable that the guest would taste the food, at least as a token of acceptance. So options 2 or 4 are preferable courses of action. Option 1 may indeed be a practical "way out" of an awkward situation; however, it does not permit the furthering of the friendship and it may be construed as rude behaviour. Similarly, option 3 also has the potential to insult the host.

Scenario 2

This scenario addresses cultural differences in conflict management. One of the best ways of finding information about appropriate social norms in a culture is to ask someone who belongs to that culture to explain these norms (this may not always be possible, but it is ideal). If a person isn't comfortable with confrontation, a collaborative conflict management style is effective. Therefore involving the other person in the situation by asking whether they can come up with a collaborative solution to an issue is good practice. Therefore, options 2 or 3 are appropriate. Option 1 may work if Ann is attuned to indirect modes of communication, but this may not be the case—further, even if Ann recognises that Wei Li has a problem, she may not know what the specific problem is. Similarly, option 4 does not communicate to Ann that Wei Li is uncomfortable with the status quo either.

Scenario 3

This scenario addresses cultural differences in styles of communication. Regardless of how pragmatic a direct style of communication may sound to a Westernised person, someone from a culture where subtlety and indirect communication are valued cannot simply switch over to a direct style, just as someone whose usual style of communication is direct cannot readily switch over to a subtle style. Therefore Omi needs a strategy that is conducive to his own style of communication (which is subtle and indirect) but somewhat accessible to Eric. Thus, options 1 or 3 provide the opportunity for the subject of Eric's incompetence in Omi's culture to be approached without requiring Omi to be confrontational. Options 2 and 4 do not facilitate the process of Eric learning about Omi's culture to rectify the situation of his offensive behaviour.

Scenario 4

Working in a different cultural environment is challenging, let alone speaking a different language. Therefore it is courteous not to put a person on the spot if their attempt at a second language is less than ideal. Option 1 allows Tom to show that just as he has trouble understanding his partner, he recognises that she too may have trouble understanding him. It is an inviting question without judgment. Option 3 provides a practical way of Tom and the partner to understand each other without being impeded by accents. Hence, either one of these options are suitable. Option 2 is an escape mechanism which prevents Tom (and his partner) from learning from this experience and isn't always practical; and option 4 may be practical but not empathetic, given Tom's partner may be embarrassed or hurt by his actions.

Assessing Intercultural Communication Competence

The process of assessing a person's intercultural communication competence requires careful thought. There are many factors to consider. For example, self-assessments may be biased by a person's misguided or idealistic sense of his/her own competence. Evaluating or assessing intercultural communication competence is usually done with the use of quantitative instruments, though there are some theoretical frameworks that are helpful for the purpose of determining the extent to which a person is developed in his/her intercultural understanding.

One such framework is the Developmental Model of Intercultural Sensitivity (DMIS). The DMIS (Bennett & Bennett, 2004) identifies six stages of development in which a person progresses from an ethnocentric state to an ethnorelative one. The ethnocentric stages are *denial*, in which a person sees his/her own culture as the only valid one, *defence*, in which one's own culture is seen as superior to that of others, and *minimisation*, in which one sees others as variations of one's own culture (thus minimising the other cultural perspectives and generalising them as resembling one's own). The ethnorelative stages are *acceptance*, where one recognises the validity and complexity of other cultures, *adaptation*, in which one is able to engage in perspective-taking by seeing things from a different cultural perspective, and *integration*, in which one's own cultural identity is influenced by the other cultural perspectives that one has encountered. The DMIS provides a useful framework with which we can evaluate the extent to which a person is ready to engage communication in intercultural spaces. This information is helpful in practical contexts such as intercultural training and education such that a trainer is able to assess the readiness of the trainees and structure the training accordingly.

Ideally, intercultural communication competence should be evaluated from the *other*'s perspective. This too, however, is complex because the very nature of intercultural communication is such that many cultural and personality variables influence the outcome of the assessment. In designing quantitative instruments that can be used across many cultures, the researcher needs to attend to certain factors. van de Vijver and Leung (1997) point out, that researchers have to account for construct, method, and item biases when designing instruments in research that involves culturally heterogeneous participants. Construct bias can arise when cultural factors influence the dimensions that are relevant to a certain construct. For example, Arasaratnam (2007) illustrates that,

> a measure of personal success may have items that allude to job satisfaction, financial security and feelings of self-worth. Perhaps such a measure would make sense to someone from an individualistic, capitalist culture. However, to someone from a collectivist or agrarian culture, parental/societal validation, family satisfaction, and progress of one's community may prove to be more relevant measures of personal success (p. 106).

Similarly, method bias can also arise due to cultural variations. The educational systems in some cultures familiarise their participants to quantitative assessment from an early age (in the form of multiple choice quizzes and tests) while this may not be the case in other cultures and hence performance in a Likert-type scale may be affected by a participant's familiarity with the concept of such an assessment. Further, item bias could arise especially when an instrument is translated not only linguistically but conceptually from one culture to another, as cultural values influence the significance people place on various concepts such as independence, extroversion, assertiveness, etc.

The ideal approach to assessment of ICC is multi-pronged, involving more than one type of measurement. The elements of assessment could include quantitative instruments for self and *other* assessment (assessment of one's ICC from the perspective of the *other*), behavioural observation, as well as qualitative contextual data.

Though the process of developing an appropriate quantitative instrument to assess ICC might present challenges, such an instrument does present a pragmatic and logistically accessible way of evaluating ICC. Using the IMICC (which was developed based on the *other's* perspective of ICC), Arasaratnam (2009) developed a quantitative instrument of ICC which consists of items that address the cognitive, affective, and behavioural dimensions. This instrument is still in its developmental stages and requires further extensive testing. Examples of some of the items from each of these dimensions from the ICC instrument are as follows:

Cognitive Dimension
1. I find it easier to categorise people based on their cultural identity than their personality.
2. I usually relate better to people with whom I have similar experiences, regardless of their cultural background.

Affective Dimension
1. I feel that people from other cultures have many valuable things to teach me.
2. I feel closer to people with whom I have a good relationship, regardless of whether they belong to my culture or not.

Behavioural Dimension
1. I usually look for opportunities to interact with people from other cultures.
2. When I communicate with someone from a different culture I usually listen more than talk.

Another instrument which evaluates a related concept to ICC is the Multicultural Personality Questionnaire (MPQ). The MPQ (van der Zee & van Oudenhoven, 2000) consists of five dimensions, specifically 1) cultural empathy (the ability to emotionally and cognitively empathise with people of other cultures), 2) open-mindedness (non judgmental, favourable attitude towards people of other cultures), 3) emotional stability (the ability to be calm in stressful situations), 4) flexibility (the ability to learn and adjust one's behaviour), and 5) social initiative (the inclination to be the initiator in social situations). The instrument has been successfully used in several studies (Leong, 2007; van Oudenhoven, Mol, & van der Zee, 2003; van Oudenhoven & van der Zee, 2002). Arasaratnam's (2006) empirical test of the IMICC utilised the cultural empathy subscale of the MPQ to measure the empathy variable in the model. The direct relationship between multicultural personality and ICC are yet to be empirically tested, but the MPQ continues to prove to be a valuable instrument in intercultural research.

Even though self-response instruments present a certain challenge in that they rely on the participants' ability to understand the question and respond accurately, evaluating ICC through behavioural observations also presents some challenges. Studies which involve observation of behaviour usually utilise a panel of coders to increase coder reliability. Even though some measures can be taken to decrease the effects of cultural biases in perception, behavioural coding as a measure of ICC is not flawless. One must avoid, however, the temptation to assume that ICC cannot possibly be assessed because of the numerous personality and contextual variables that influence ICC. This is a simplistic assumption based on the premise that there are no generalisable patterns of behaviour—a premise that any social scientist would refute. ICC can indeed be assessed. However, as mentioned before, measurement of ICC should ideally involve multiple techniques.

Factors that Debilitate Communication in Intercultural Spaces

Just as the variables identified in the IMICC contribute to someone being perceived as a competent intercultural communicator, there are certain other variables which debilitate one's ability to competently communicate in intercultural spaces. Though there are several such variables that can be identified, three pertinent variables are discussed in this section, all three of which can be characterised as orientations or attitudes that colour one's interactions with people who are perceived as the *other*.

Prejudice

Prejudice is an attitude or predisposition toward a person or a group of people. Though prejudice can be negative or positive, we often think of prejudice in terms of the negative. Allport (1954), for example, characterises negative prejudice as, "an aversive or hostile attitude toward a person who belongs to a group; simply because he belongs to that group; and it is, therefore, presumed to have the objectionable qualities ascribed to the group" (p. 7). Racism, or racial prejudice, is a form of prejudice that is particularly relevant in intercultural spaces. *Race* is a socially constructed label used to describe a group of people who are visually similar based on certain physical attributes that are selected as important markers (such as skin colour, hair colour, facial features, etc.). De Lima Nunes and colleagues (2010) claim, "prejudice will be the result of institutional processes of differentiation according to skin colour and the phenotype features that still exist today" (p. 5).

Negative prejudice can be debilitating in intercultural spaces because people who are very prejudiced are resistant to information that contradicts their prejudicial beliefs (Gudykunst & Kim, 2003) and are therefore not disposed to open communication with members of the group toward which they are prejudiced. Even if they come across someone from that group who behaves in a way that completely contradicts the prejudicial attributes associated with that group, prejudiced individuals are likely to ignore this contradiction.

Prejudice is hard to change because it serves certain socio-cognitive needs. Brislin (1979) identifies four key functions of prejudice, namely, the function of being perceived favourably by members of our ingroup who may also hold the same prejudicial attitudes (*utilitarian* function), the function of protecting our self-image by giving us someone else to blame in the face of our failures (*ego-defensive* function), the function of defining the values of our own group by identifying what we are not (*value-expressive* function), and the function of helping us categorise and organise people in our mind (*knowledge* function).

Discrimination occurs when prejudicial attitudes translate into behaviour based on these attitudes. For example, a driving instructor might have the prejudicial attitude that he doesn't like Asians, based on the stereotypical belief that Asians are bad drivers. If that instructor then proceeds to fail an Asian student in a driving test that any other non-Asian student would have passed, then his behaviour is discriminatory.

Though it may be hard to change prejudicial attitudes, it is not impossible. In his *Contact Hypothesis*, Allport (1954) proposed that prejudice can be reduced through intergroup contact under conditions of equal status, intergroup cooperation, presence of common goals, and support from relevant social institutions. The Contact Hypothesis has been empirically tested extensively since Allport's initial proposal (Pettigrew & Tropp, 2006; Tredoux & Finchilescu, 2007). There is even some evidence to suggest that attitudes could be altered based on imagined contact with the target group. Turner and Crisp (2010), for example, found that participants who imagined interacting with a certain people group showed positive attitudes toward that group of people merely based on this imagined contact.

Prejudice and the discriminatory behaviour that often results from it can foster feelings of resentment and misunderstanding in intercultural spaces. Thus prejudice can hinder effective and appropriate communication in such instances. Another attitude that debilitates communication in intercultural spaces is ethnocentrism.

Ethnocentrism

One of the earliest definitions of *ethnocentrism* is by Sumner (1906), who defined it as, "this view of things in which one's own group is the centre of everything, and all others are scaled and rated with reference to it" (p. 13). Ethnocentrism is associated with feeling as well as belief. Ethnocentric individuals evaluate other worldviews/perspectives from the assumption that their own point of view is the central and/or superior one. Ethnocentrism thus distorts an alternative worldview within the ethical and moral parameters of one's own culture. Neuliep, Hintz, and McCroskey (2005) explain:

> Attitudinally, ethnocentric persons see the ingroup as superior to outgroups. Behaviourally, ethnocentric persons foster cooperative relations with ingroup members while competing with, and perhaps even battling, with outgroup members (p. 42).

Because of their predisposition to evaluate other people's cultural perspective based on the values of their own culture, ethnocentric individuals are likely to misjudge others and misconstrue messages in intercultural spaces. In a study to test the predictors of anxiety or apprehension associated with interacting with people (communication apprehension) from a different ethnicity, Toale and McCroskey (2001) found that ethnocentrism was a strong predictor of interethnic communication apprehension.

Unlike prejudice, which is directed toward particular groups of people, ethnocentrism is more pervasive. Ethnocentrism prompts one to evaluate every other group against the values and beliefs of one's own group. This can debilitate communication in intercultural spaces because an ethnocentric individual is inherently unable to engage in the exercise of perspective-taking that is so vital to effective and appropriate intercultural communication, as illustrated by the IMICC. Beyond debilitating everyday intercultural exchanges, ethnocentrism can also fuel attitudes that have far greater consequences. In their discussion of the role of ethnocentrism on America's "war on terrorism," Kam and Kinder (2007) explain:

> To most Americans, the adversaries in this war are unfamiliar. They come from far away and exotic places. Their language, religion, customs, and sheer physical appearance: all of it is strange. After 9/11, not just strange, but sinister. Americans who are generally predisposed towards ethnocentrism—who as a matter of habit see the world divided into virtuous ingroups and inferior outgroups—should be especially likely to lend their support to the new war on terrorism (p. 323).

It is inevitable that all of us are ethnocentric to an extent because we cannot help but be influenced by the cultural perspective with which we are most familiar. Neuliep and McCroskey (1997) argue that:

> The concept of ethnocentrism is essentially descriptive and not necessarily pejorative. . . Ethnocentrism forms the basis of patriotism and the willingness to sacrifice for one's central group (p. 389).

In increased doses, however, ethnocentrism can lead to apathy or hostility toward other cultures. While studying the relationship between sensation seeking and the formation of intercultural friendships, Arasaratnam and Banerjee (2007) discovered that the introduction of ethnocentrism into the model of sensation seeking and variables that influence intercultural contact-seeking behaviour reduced the strength of relationships between all the variables. In other words, a high sensation seeker was more motivated to seek intercultural friendships in the absence of ethnocentrism (in the model) than in the presence of it. Ethnocentrism thus acts as a debilitating agent in intercultural spaces.

Existential Insecurity

The third factor which debilitates communication in intercultural spaces is what I'd characterise as an existential fear or insecurity in which a person feels threatened by people or groups of people who hold different values and beliefs. The label of existential insecurity has been used to describe a condition of material poverty and lack of a sense of wellbeing, in other literature (Rindfleisch, Burroughs, & Wong, 2008; Thomas, 2007). I am, however, using this label as a condition in which one feels threatened by alternative worldviews.

This notion is related to the idea of culture serving as a means of symbolic immortality, as in the context of the *Terror Management Theory* which was discussed in Chapter 2. If people see culture as a means of achieving symbolic immortality, then it stands to reason that they would find alternative cultural worldviews threatening, especially if they feel that the existence of alternative worldviews pollutes or diminishes the integrity of their own worldview.

I was once conducting an intercultural training seminar in which a participant asked whether I was promoting a type of cultural pluralism in which homogenous unique cultures no longer existed. The subscript of the question was that unless cultural groups vigilantly guard against outside influences, they will lose their uniqueness and integrity. This question reflects a valid and real fear of losing one's cultural identity to the morphing and blending of cultural values that often follows extensive contact with another culture. There are two ways of responding to such a question. First, the transformation of a culture over time is inevitable. If anyone needs convincing of this, they simply need to study history. Modernisation and the influx of global media, among other things, contribute to change in any homogenous culture. This is evident in generational differences in understanding of concepts such as politeness, modesty, respect, etc. even within a particular cultural context. Hence it is unrealistic for one to expect one's present cultural values to remain unchanged over time. Secondly, the question of whether contact with other cultures will pollute one's own culture is based on the assumption that one cannot remain faithful to one's own cultural values while interacting closely with people from another culture. This assumption may indeed be valid to an extent, given we as social beings are influenced by one another as we symbolically co-create meaning. However, this process of co-creation of meaning between cultural entities does not necessarily have to be perceived as a threat. An individual who is existentially secure would perceive it as an opportunity instead—an opportunity to expand one's schematic framework of reference.

Existential insecurity debilitates communication in intercultural spaces because it prevents people from seeing culturally different others as individuals from whom one can learn and with whom one can co-create social meaning. Existential insecurity gives one the false impression that one has no agency in the meaning making process—it fuels the fear that if one associates with a culturally different other, then the other person would somehow hijack the process of meaning making such that the end result will be a new social reality in which one's own cultural values are obsolete.

Thus prejudice, ethnocentrism, and a sense of fear based on existential insecurity can debilitate communication in intercultural spaces, just as the ability to empathise and listen, and the motivation to interact with people from other cultures fuelled by positive attitudes toward other cultures, enhance communication in intercultural spaces.

Concluding Thoughts

Communication in intercultural spaces is adventurous, complex, and potentially richly rewarding. Intercultural spaces challenge our ability to look beyond our own perspective and invite us to see the world—and even see ourselves—as someone else does. As the stories in the next chapter illustrate, intercultural communication is intricately woven into the day-to-day experiences of those of us who live in culturally diverse communities.

One of the main aims of this book is to challenge the reader to consider the social cognitive processes that are so fundamental to our everyday operations through the lens of intercultural communication. Our perceptions so pervasively influence our reactions to people and situations such that a student of intercultural communication cannot afford not to systematically study perceptual processes. When encountered with someone whom we perceive as blatantly racist or prejudiced, it is often tempting to pummel them with fact after fact to dispute what appear as irrational and ignorant views. Perhaps some of us have even tried this and, much to our frustration and incredulity, realised that the other person simply dismissed our well-construed arguments as irrelevant. These are the instances where a richer understanding of perceptual processes enables us to thoughtfully address the deeper issues that under gird overt racist or prejudiced behaviour.

Historic events have taught us that on the one hand the presence of various kinds of fears such as fear of the unknown, fear of becoming obsolete, fear of competing for resources, fear of losing one's identity, etc., prevent people from being open to understanding the perspective of the culturally different *other*; and on the other hand ignorance prevents some of us from realising that the real threat is our own fear—not the presence of the *other*. When faced with our fears, it is easy to find someone to blame or someone to avoid because it gives us a sense of control and deludes us into thinking that we are taking measures to eliminate the cause of our fears. But this sort of impulsive reaction robs us of the opportunity for meta-reflection and enrichment through intercultural dialogue. Fear is a hard obstacle to overcome. Ignorance, on the other hand, is arguably curable! It is my hope that the thoughts shared in this book would be one among the many such sources of cure for ignorance.

Chapter Six
EVERYDAY INTERCULTURAL SPACES

Though fundamentally based on several real-life experiences, these short stories are fictitious. Their purpose, as explained in the introduction, is to highlight intercultural concepts in everyday interactions with the subtlety that is characteristic of most everyday encounters. The short stories can be used as teaching aids or instruments to generate discussion. Their main purpose, however, is to engage the reader to reflect on the theoretical concepts discussed in previous chapters as they apply to daily interactions in intercultural spaces.

Story 1: Bad Day

Darren was having a bad day. It all started with his meeting at the registrar's office. No, it all started with the headache with which he had woken this morning. It was one of those dull, persistent throbbing headaches that wasn't too demanding to warrant much attention if you are very busy, but not too subtle that you could totally ignore it. Darren was busy, so he ignored it nevertheless.

His alarm had failed to go off at 7AM as it should have. He hadn't gotten good sleep in the first place because the black guys who lived next door had been playing their loud music again till well past midnight. Darren had gotten dressed in a hurry and rushed out the door without pausing for breakfast or even his usual cup of morning coffee, only to discover that he had missed the campus bus which would have taken him to the registrar's office a few minutes before the meeting. He ran all the way, and arrived seven minutes late. Fortunately one of the assistant registrars was still available to assist him, and he had walked up to her, panting slightly and sweating profusely even though it was still chilly outside on that cold February morning in New Jersey.

Darren needed to graduate in May, because he knew his parents who had a small farm in Idaho could not pay for another term's tuition. The part-time job he had at the campus bookstore was barely enough to cover his rent and regular supply of Ramen noodles and coffee. He had put in a request with the registrar's office for some of the credits from the community college classes he had taken a while ago to be transferred toward his degree. When he had spoken about this with someone at the office on a previous occasion, they had assured him that the credits would transfer. Today, however, the assistant registrar gave him the unwelcome news that the credits would not transfer after all. Darren had pointed out that he had been told previously that they would transfer, reasoned that he needed the extra two classes to graduate in May, and pleaded that he couldn't afford to study another term—to no avail. The assistant registrar suggested that Darren could take the two remaining classes in the summer term and still graduate before Fall term, though his official certificate would not be issued till much later. Darren had walked out of the registrar's office dejectedly, only to discover that he was already ten minutes late for his next class.

He ran across campus once more, arriving frazzled and fifteen minutes late to the seminar room where Dr. Zedwick was discussing McLuhan. Fortunately Darren was able to slip into the classroom at the precise moment when Dr. Zedwick's head was turned toward the whiteboard, thus avoiding one of Dr. Z's caustic remarks that were typically directed at latecomers.

The headache made itself known again. Darren rubbed his temples and tried to concentrate on the distinction between hot and cool media. How was he supposed to pay for summer school? He couldn't work any more hours than he already did, given he was barely keeping up with his studies as it was. Could he borrow money from Uncle Jay? His mother's brother lived in New York, and had often offered to be of help to Darren should he need it. But Darren had not asked anything of his uncle because he didn't want to be an imposition.

With a sigh, Darren realised that asking Uncle Jay for help was the only course of action. Of course, Darren would work out a timeline to pay off the money he borrowed. He hoped Uncle Jay was in town—he knew Jay travelled extensively for his work, sometimes being out of the country for months at a time. Darren decided he'd call Jay during one of his breaks at work that afternoon.

Class had ended before Darren had properly caught on to the subject of discussion, and he wearily walked out of the building only to realise that, in his haste that morning, he had left his jacket at home. He hadn't realised how cold it was because he had been running everywhere. But now, as flurries wafted in the cold February wind, Darren shivered. There was no time to go home and get his jacket. He was scheduled to do a double shift at the bookstore before his evening class which Dr. Kim had (despite much protests and groans from the students) scheduled at the last minute, to make up for a session they had missed during the previous week due to an extended fire drill.

Wrapping his arms around his body against the freezing wind, Darren hurried to the bookstore. His stomach growled. It was almost lunchtime and he hadn't eaten anything yet. There was no time to stop for food, but he figured he could eat something at his break.

The bookstore was unusually crowded for a Thursday. The assistant manager was looking harassed. She impatiently gestured at Darren to hurry up and assume his post. The first half of his shift passed in a blur. Darren was grateful when it was finally time for his first fifteen minute break. He desperately needed to eat something, but he decided to place a quick call to Uncle Jay first, to ease his mind.

He got Jay's secretary (after being put on hold for nearly ten minutes) who informed him that Jay was in a meeting. Instead of leaving a message, Darren decided to call later. A swift glance at his watch told him that he didn't have time to run to the cafeteria and back before he had to return to his post. The headache had now grown in confidence to sharp throbs.

In the second part of his shift Darren had to deal with three different bad tempered customers. One was a large black lady who was insisting that she should get a full refund for a book that was damaged, while not being able to substantiate that she had purchased that book from the campus bookstore. The assistant manager fortunately stepped in and relieved Darren of having to deal with that customer further. The second bad tempered customer was a freshman, probably eighteen or nineteen by the look of her pale white face, who was trying to pass off one of the notebooks she had lifted from the store as her own. The alarm kept going off every time she tried to leave the store and she kept screaming and insisting that she was being harassed. She calmed down quickly when she saw a campus police officer walking by and stalked off, looking very offended, having slammed the notebook in question on the counter. The third bad tempered customer was a severe-looking Asian professor who was probably having a bad day like Darren, and, to Darren's dismay, the cash machine simply froze when he was serving this customer. He could not complete the purchase because there were codes and receipts involved and he didn't want to do anything before he got assistance from the manager. But as the manager was on the phone, he had to wait for a while, throwing desperate glances in the direction of the manager, and listening to the professor's diatribe about the inefficiency of campus services.

By the time he got off work it was 5PM and nearly dark outside. He still had not eaten for the day, because the store was so busy that he had not had a chance to think about anything else. The headache was raging in full force now. It felt like someone was hitting his head with a large mallet. His hands almost froze instantly as he stepped out of the heated bookstore into the frigid evening. His stomach was burning with hunger. Every muscle in his body ached from the long hours of standing and running around in the bookstore. He even contemplated ditching Dr. Kim's supplementary class, but quickly decided against it because Dr. Kim had hinted that there might be an "impromptu" quiz that night. He had precisely half an hour before he had to be in class.

The closest cafeteria officially closed at 5PM, but there were usually people still eating till about 5:10. If he hurried, he might just be able to snag a slice of pizza before they put all the food away. He knew he could not go on any longer without eating. He nearly felt faint with hunger and headache in addition to feeling dejected about not getting his credits transferred, not being able to graduate in May, not having his jacket, and not being able to reach Uncle Jay yet.

Mustering the remains of his energy, Darren hurried to the cafeteria, ducking once more against the ferocious cold wind. It was warm inside the cafeteria, for which Darren was immensely grateful. He hastened to the counter, looking around in dismay and realising that the place was nearly deserted. A single black man was scraping the remains of the food from the grill, clearly cleaning up for the night.

Disappointment flooded into Darren with such force that he was nearly in tears. Could this day get any worse? Why, oh why, had he not eaten something before? Anything! Maybe even a pack of M&Ms from the bookstore! The backpack slid from his shoulder onto the floor as he sighed wearily and rubbed his throbbing temples.

"Can I help you?" the black man asked, clearly having heard the thump of the backpack dropping to the floor.

Darren sighed. "I guess not . . . I'd hoped to get here before you closed, but . . ." he looked down and dejectedly picked up the backpack.

"You knew we close at 5, didn't you?"

Darren glanced up wearily. He wasn't in the mood for a "next time you should know better" lecture. Darren focused on the man behind the counter. He was probably in his late thirties, tall and muscular, wearing a white T-shirt and a white apron around his waist over the faded blue jeans. He was frowning slightly and his dark eyes were focused on Darren, waiting for an answer.

"I was working till just now," Darren said, a little defensively. "And usually I just go home for dinner, but I've a class tonight and I didn't get to eat all day and . . . " he left the words trail, wondering why he was standing around bothering to explain himself when he could be using the remaining few precious minutes before class to swing by a vending machine. His headache was nearly unbearable now, and his stomach was on fire with hunger.

The black man nodded thoughtfully. "OK, what would you like to eat?"

Darren stared in surprise. "Aren't you closed? Weren't you just cleaning the grill?"

"Yes," he replied. Then his dark face broke into a wide grin. "But we're here to serve the students, right? Here you are, a student, desperately needing food, so I'm gonna fix you something to eat! So what's it gonna be?"

Darren, having experienced a whole day of bureaucracy, bad tempers, and mishaps, was stunned by the unexpected kindness of the cafeteria worker. In that moment of wonder his mind raced through the facts that the worker probably would have to stay later than his shift to cook Darren's food and clean up afterwards and probably would get home later than usual on this cold night, perhaps would have to miss whatever plans he had for the evening—and yet here he was, offering a meal to an arguably irritable student, even though he was well within his right to close shop and head out as he would've done otherwise.

Darren was overwhelmed with gratitude.

"I . . . I'd love a burger, if it isn't too much trouble," Darren managed to say.

The black man quickly relit the grill and got to work on Darren's burger. "How's your day so far?" he called over his shoulder, making polite conversation with Darren.

The meat hit the grill with a sizzle and the glorious fragrance of browning beef made Darren's stomach rumble in anticipation. Even his headache seemed to have dulled, as if resigning to its demise now that food was imminent. He watched the tall man spread delectable sauces on a fresh bun with experienced swiftness.

Darren smiled. "It just got better."

Interview with Darren

Lily: Hello Darren. What's it like to be a college student in Jersey?

Darren: It's a lot of fun—well, most of the time, anyway!

Lily: What do you enjoy the most about the experience?

Darren: I like this city because you come across all kinds of people from all over the world, and that's quite a novelty for a country boy from Idaho.

Lily: So, you enjoy the cultural diversity on campus?

Darren: Yeah, sure! Like I have this guy from China in my class and he was saying that he'd never heard of General Tzo's chicken before he came to the US! Crazy, eh?

Lily: It sounds like you're having fun interacting with new people. Is it difficult to be amongst people from various ethnicities after growing up in a predominantly white town?

Darren: Not really. I like getting to know different people. I've noticed some things about different groups, actually. Like the Asians tend to be quiet unless they're talking to their own kind, and then they tend to be cliquey like that, the Italians tend to be loud but friendly, the Latinos are friendly as well, and black people tend to be loud and often stick with their own kind too.

Lily: Those are interesting observations. Darren, I wonder if we could talk for a bit about stereotypes and prejudice.

Darren: That's an unusual subject to bring up—sure, why not.

Lily: Do you consider yourself a prejudiced person?

Darren: No, I don't think so. I mean I don't make rude racist jokes or discriminate against anyone based on their colour or anything—I assume you're talking about racial prejudice?

Lily: Yes. Do you ever assign a set of qualities to a group of people?

Darren: You mean stereotype? Yeah, I guess so. Like these black guys in my neighbourhood—they're always playing loud music, and these black kids in my classes are always talking loudly. So I tend to think black people are loud like I said before. I guess that's a stereotype.

Lily: And what does that mean to you? To be loud, that is?

Darren: I think that's inconsiderate. Because the neighbours keep me up with their music—and that's pretty inconsiderate, and the guys in the class talk loud without thinking they're disturbing the other students. I even had this black lady customer one time that yelled loudly and made a scene—pretty inconsiderate.

Lily: So you're saying that certain specific observations of black people being "loud" has lead you to a generalised belief that black people in general are loud, thus creating a stereotype, and because you believe that being loud is inconsiderate, you are therefore predisposed to thinking that black people are inconsiderate?

Darren: Well . . . that's a bit of a stretch but not much of a stretch . . . yes; it is in essence true—though I never really thought about it that way. Wow! I guess I've been prejudiced without really realising it!

Lily: Many of us are. Has any black person violated your prejudiced expectation of this group?

Darren: Yes! When I went to the cafeteria the other day after having a really bad day all around, I was dejected when I saw the black man behind the counter. I guess subconsciously I didn't expect him to be kind to me. Because my neighbours are rude, the black lady in the shop was rude, and in general I guess I've only noticed rude behaviour from black people—but this guy was so different! His kindness really took me by surprise—it stood in stark contrast to the rest of the day.

Lily: Is it possible that you only noticed "rudeness" from black people because of your stereotype of them? Is it also possible that you noticed the cafeteria man's kindness because it stood out dramatically in a day that had mostly gone wrong?

Darren: Yes . . . and yes. Wow, I never thought about it that way. I don't mean to be a prejudiced person—or someone who judges other people simply based on stereotypes. But I guess subconsciously I've been acting that way. I really need to think about this. . . . I remember learning in class about the conversion model of stereotype change. I don't think my experience was very dramatic, but I still feel like something has changed inside me since I met that kind cafeteria worker.

Lily: Are you saying you are revising your stereotype of black people?

Darren: Definitely! I mean, I know that in any group of people there are some general patterns or kinds of behaviour—there has to be, right? I mean there are similarities in the way people who're from a similar background or who're raised in a similar way behave, aren't there? But I guess I have to keep in mind that there are many exceptions to these generalisations and be careful not to always try to fit people into those boxes. I'm still learning.

Lily: Well, "still learning" better than "not teachable!" Keep on learning.

Story 2: Arranged Marriage

Shruti awoke to the smell of flowers, sandalwood, and cooking, and the sound of laughter. Before she could get out of bed her cousin Lalitha came bounding into the room and jumped on the bed.

"Wake up, sleepy head! Don't waste the last hours of your freedom sleeping away!" She giggled and tickled Shruti into submission as she resisted her attempts to pull her out of bed.

"OK, OK, I'm up," Shruti said, sitting up and stretching. "What's all the commotion outside?"

"Uncle Raman and family just arrived and your Mum's cooking breakfast for the battalion. You better hurry up and get ready. We have to be at the church in an hour.

Shruti glanced at her reflection in the mirror before stepping into the shower. It was her wedding day. This evening I will be Mrs. Abraham, she thought. I would never be Shruti Jacobs again after 1:30PM today.

Breakfast was a hurried and chaotic affair as relatives kept coming and going, taking care of last minute details and making sure all the cars were loaded with the necessary items. Once at the church, Shruti and her bridesmaids started getting ready in the dressing room, assisted by several aunts and cousins. She caught a glimpse of her mother from time to time, who was running around making sure everything was in order.

Shruti flinched as Aunt Saratha pulled at a strand of her long hair. "Oops! Sorry dear," she apologised. "Your hair is all tangled. Let's comb it out before we style it."

As Aunt Saratha worked on her hair, Shruti let her mind wander to the previous couple of months. She had just arrived from America, having completed her Masters degree in Engineering. She had come home to visit her parents before returning to assume a new job. It was great to be back in India. She had missed the smell of spices everywhere, the crowded streets with three-wheelers and motorbikes and every other vehicle imaginable, and she had definitely missed her mother's cooking. Even though she knew the matter of her marriage would come up if she returned home, she couldn't resist coming home for a visit.

Her relatives had lost no time in bringing up the subject of marriage. "You are twenty seven already. You shouldn't wait any longer," they had said. She realised her parents had been under a lot of pressure from the relatives too, regarding her single status. All her female cousins of "marriageable age" were already married. Shruti had indeed thought of marriage from time to time, but she just had not met the right man yet. It was not, however, due to the lack of male suitors.

Ever since she was young Shruti seemed to attract men without trying. She had one of those faces that was so stunningly beautiful that it made anyone turn around for a second look. But most people who long for beauty don't know that such extraordinary beauty comes as a great burden to a young person who is just trying to fit in. Shruti always wanted to be an engineer. While her ten year old friends were playing with dolls and throwing imaginary tea parties, Shruti played with the circuit board she had constructed with the small motor, bulbs and wires her uncle had given her from his utility shop. She was so determined to do well in school that she was irritated by the constant efforts of her male classmates to get her attention. Between that and her female classmates' reluctance to befriend her because of their insecurity with their own appearance, Shruti was mostly a loner while growing up. Now, as an adult, she felt that things were not much different from when she was younger. Whenever a man would befriend her, she was not sure whether it was out of interest in her as a person or because he was just smitten with her appearance. Hardly any of her male colleagues had taken her seriously as an engineer, till she out performed them in every class. No matter how much her relatives tried to convince her, the idea of an arranged marriage was not appealing. She was tired of dealing with the same type of men all her life and the last thing she wanted to do was to parade herself in front of potential suitors just so that they could start gushing about how beautiful she was without even bothering to get to know her as a person.

Even though her parents did not pressure her regarding marriage, she knew they were worried about her. She felt guilty about causing that worry. But she couldn't help not having met the right man yet. She had many friends who had fallen in love with the man of their dreams and had raved about how great that was. She didn't know what that was like, but it sounded good.

It was both painful and humiliating to be constantly reminded by her relatives that she was getting older and if she did not hurry up, nobody would want to marry her. She had overheard too many whispers behind her back. "Ah, pity! She's so beautiful! I wonder why nobody has married her yet . . ." "She must be stubborn. You know, our girls when they go abroad to study they become Westernised and hard headed. That's why I will never send my daughter abroad." "I hear she is an engineer. I wonder what her parents were thinking . . . it's such a manly profession. No wonder she isn't married. Such a shame . . . I guess beauty doesn't mean anything unless you are raised properly. . . "

She had agreed to meet with Arun just to silence those whispers. She thought if she met some potential suitors then the relatives would at least be satisfied that she had tried. Arun was the son of one of her uncle's friends. She was told that he was also based in America, and was in town for holiday. Their meeting was to take place in a coffee shop near her parents' home.

Shruti had hardly put any effort into getting dressed for that meeting. She had already made up her mind that she would politely but firmly explain to Arun that she was not interested in an arranged marriage, but that she was happy to make a new acquaintance. She figured he would understand, given he too must be familiar with the concept of marriages that weren't arranged!

She had found him waiting for her at the table when she showed up. He was tall and had a friendly face. He greeted her with impeccable manners and they sat down to a pleasant conversation. They talked about what they did in America, how long they had been away from home, and about the kinds of things they had missed about India. She found out that Arun was a computer programmer for Intel. Neither one of them brought up the subject of marriage.

This whole situation is weird, she thought. She wasn't even sure what she was doing there. He was pleasant enough to talk to, but it was bizarre to think that she was supposed to be evaluating the stranger across the table as her potential husband.

Taking a long sip from his second cup of coffee, Arun said, "So, what would you look for in your husband?" taking her completely off guard.

Shruti almost choked on her coffee. "Um . . . what?"

"Well, aren't we here to find out whether we'd like to marry each other?"

She had looked up to find him looking at her with a twinkle in his eyes. He seemed to be amused by her shock at the abrupt change of topic.

"Well," she had said, quickly regaining her composure, "I would like to be with a man who is honourable, who respects his parents, respects me, and who shares my spiritual beliefs." She decided to turn the tables on him. "And how about you? What are you looking for in a wife?"

"Oh, she should definitely be able to beat me at chess. Apart from that, everything is negotiable."

She stared at him incredulously, before realising that he was teasing her.

"One's abilities at chess are very important," he continued, "but I do want a wife who is heading in the same direction as I am, spiritually, emotionally, and in terms of goals in life. I'd like to be with someone who captures my attention and keeps me amazed every day."

For the first time, Shruti noticed that he had very dark brown eyes, like rich chocolate. They were still focused on her face.

"For example, I noticed that right before you entered the shop you stopped to give the beggar seated by the door some money, and you smiled at him. I noticed that whenever you glance at the baby in the next booth your face completely relaxes and you have a smile, and I noticed that you smiled at our waitress when she took our order. You were kind to her when she dropped her tray. I noticed that you smile when you speak about your work and when you speak about your parents. And I also noticed that you haven't smiled at me yet once."

Shruti was stunned. She had expected him to compliment her on her looks, to gush about how he could make her happy, or to feign interest in her work while staring absently at her face. But she had not expected this.

"I'm sorry," she had said, looking down at the milky surface of her coffee. "It wasn't fair of me to agree to this meeting, especially when I had already made up my mind about how it would conclude."

"Why did you agree to come then?"

She sighed. What should she tell him? That she was just trying to silence her relatives? That she was tired of superficial men who could not see her as an intelligent person and therefore she had had no expectation of him being any different? That she did not want to offend her uncle's friend?

"I see. You just agreed to meet me so that your relatives won't keep hassling you about marriage," he had said, as if reading her mind. "I have a sister," he said simply, when she stared in surprise.

"Let me make this easy on you," he had said after a moment's silence. "I am looking for someone who is intelligent, kind, and can share my life with me as my partner and friend. Ideally, I'd like to get to know her before we decide whether we want to get married. I had not planned on meeting with you—or any other women, for that matter, for the purpose of finding a potential wife. But my father asked me to meet you, and I didn't want to be disrespectful. I figured at the very least I could make a friend with whom I could talk about our experiences in America. That's why I came."

He paused to set his cup of coffee down. "I would still like the opportunity to have that friendship, if you too would like that. And, once we get to know each other a little better, if we find that we could pursue a deeper relationship that could lead to marriage, then I am open to that. But I don't want to keep you here any longer if this isn't something you'd like to do." He pulled out his wallet and set a few notes of money on the table. "I am planning to come here for a cup of coffee tomorrow afternoon, around three. If you would like to get to know me, feel free to join me." With that, he stood up and waited for her, indicating that the conversation was over, before Shruti could think of what to say.

Shruti was so taken in by his candour that she had decided to give this friendship a chance. They had spent most of the following month getting to know each other, and were surprised to discover that they not only had a lot of values in common but also thoroughly enjoyed each other's company.

Shruti wasn't sure whether this was what her friends meant when they raved about falling in love. But she was sure that if she were to get married, she wanted to marry someone like Arun who was honest, kind, fun to be with, and made her feel like a beautiful woman in a way that was quite different from the ogling to which she was accustomed. They had developed a mutual respect and attraction for each other. Everyone was delighted when they decided to get married.

"So is this an arranged marriage or not?" her American friend Claire had asked, when Shruti had phoned her to convey the good news.

"I honestly don't know," Shruti had replied, after thinking for a moment.

* * *

"Oh you look so beautiful!" Lalitha complimented. Shruti smiled in response, and took her place in the bridal procession.

"Don't worry, dear," her father said, patting her hand, "I'll make sure I'll hold you firmly so you won't trip on your train." He winked at her with a smile.

The organ music started, and the procession began. Shruti looked ahead through the lacy fabric of her veil. All the way at the end of the aisle she saw the tall form of Arun, looking handsome in his tuxedo. He was smiling. As she started walking toward the alter, she was glad that Arun was the man who was waiting for her at the end of the aisle. She briefly reflected on her conversation with Claire again.

"But how do you know you want to marry him? After all, you've only known each other for about a month. How do you know he won't turn out to be the wrong man?"

"I don't," Shruti had replied. "But neither does everyone else who ever gets married—regardless of whether they had an arranged marriage or not. You just choose your partner wisely and commit to working on your marriage."

"It doesn't sound romantic at all," Claire had complained. "It sounds too practical. I just want to make sure you're not just settling for something less than the ideal."

"I'm not," Shruti had assured her. "If I were settling, I would've married the first man my relatives ever suggested and saved myself years of berating!"

The music ceased as she came to a halt next to Arun. He smiled and took her hand. Shruti felt an inexplicable excitement at the new adventure on which they were about to embark.

Interview with Shruti and Claire

Lily: Hello, Shruti, Claire. Shruti, congratulations on your marriage!

Shruti: Thank you!

Claire: I still don't understand how she could meet a man and marry him within a month!

Lily: Can you explain why?
Claire: Well, marriage is supposed to be the meeting of hearts. You get to know one another, you fall in love, and then you get married. The whole idea of meeting someone for the first time under the premise of "suitor selection" is strange!

Shruti: I agree to an extent, but how do we know what marriage is "supposed to be?" I mean, aren't marriages done differently in each culture?

Lily: Good point. You're alluding to the whole idea of schemata. We have a conceptual framework of what something is supposed to be, based on our cultural understanding of it. So, Claire, being raised in a white American family, has a certain conceptualisation of marriage which is different from the one which your parents and relatives have, Shruti. For them, I imagine, a perfect marriage is one that is perfectly arranged and orchestrated such that it is a meeting of suitable families. Is that correct?

Shruti: Right on!

Claire: But then who's right? These are very different "conceptualisations," as you call it, of the same concept!

Lily: Shruti, what do you think?

Shruti: I don't think there is a right or wrong in this case. Having lived in two cultures, I've noticed that there are cultural differences in the conceptualisation of many social concepts. For example, in India a fair skinned woman is considered more beautiful than a dark skinned one—mind you, we're all dark compared to Caucasians! But my white American friends spend hours at the tanning salon just so they could have a brown complexion. So, the ideal for beauty is culturally constructed. Who has the "correct" interpretation of beauty? I don't think that matters. What matters is that we need to be aware of how a particular culture sees the world so that we can understand the values of the people and operate accordingly.

Claire: OK, the varying perceptions in beauty are something I understand—because "beauty is in the eyes of the beholder," right? But I still have a problem with this idea of arranged marriages. It seems so unromantic and even a little unjust!

Shruti: In some situations that may well be the case—I know of friends who're from very traditional families where the parents selected their partners for them and really gave them no choice in the matter. But in my case it was a bit different. Arun and I were of the same mind in that we wanted to get to know each other before deciding whether we should marry, and so it worked out well for us. But the idea of arranged marriages worked really well in the olden days when families lived in close proximity to one another and everyone knew everyone else; and therefore parents could make informed judgments about who would be a good suitor for their child. But now we live very transient lives. So it is no longer practical to operate under the same rules when you're trying to arrange a marriage between two people who live in different countries and two families who may have never met one another.

Claire: Ah! So you're admitting that arranged marriages today are no longer appropriate?

Shruti: I didn't say that. I'd like to make a distinction between the *concept* and the *process*. The concept of an arranged marriage isn't something with which I disagree. I think it has evolved over the years in particular cultural contexts, and therefore I just see it as a certain perspective on the concept of marriage—a particular schema of marriage, if you will, to put it as Lily did. But I don't agree with the process of it as it is done today, at least most of the time, because I think you can't apply the same principles which worked under certain social conditions to a different world which operates under different social conditions. In my case, however, the process worked because Arun and I were given the opportunity to engage the process in a way that was appropriate to the socio-cultural conditions under which we operate.

Claire: Wow, who would've thought she's an engineer? She knows how to use words, doesn't she?

Lily: She does indeed! And she has, as precisely as only an engineer could, made an important distinction between concept and process, while highlighting the importance of recognising cultural influences on schemata. Well done!

Claire: I'm not sure whether I fully understand this whole arranged marriage thing, but I think I at least understand a bit more about where Shruti's coming from. I'll try to keep an open mind.

Shruti: That's a key ingredient in intercultural dialogue, don't you agree, Lily?

Lily: I sure do!

Story 3: Coming Home

David was nervous. He looked out the window at the dusty road ahead, as the crowded bus crawled toward the security checkpoint. He could see armed guards interrogating the driver of the vehicle ahead. Some guards were sitting on stacks of sandbags, staring blankly. They looked no older than twenty. David checked his backpack to ensure he had all his documents. He had heard many horror stories about these checkpoints and he didn't want any trouble.

The bus came to a jerky halt and three guards thundered aboard, their AK 47s slung around their shoulders like menacing extra appendages. "Papers!" Everyone held out their documents as the guards walked down the aisle. David noticed that his hand was shaking as he held up his. His heart skipped a beat when one of the guards came to a stop in front of him. "You. Where're you from?"

"Canada. I'm coming to visit my grandmother."

"Open your bag," he prodded David's backpack with his gun.

As he inspected the contents of his backpack, David wondered what had alerted the guard to the fact that he wasn't a local. Seeming satisfied with the inspection, the guard moved on and within a few more minutes all three guards got off and the bus resumed its slow sojourn along the bumpy road.

"They must be in a hurry today," called the driver, yelling to be heard above the noisy engine. "They didn't even ask anyone to get off for inspection."

David realised he had been holding his breath till the guards got off. He let out a long sigh. The little girl in the next seat was squirming again, clearly tired from the long journey. "Shh . . . ," her mother said in a consoling tone. "We'll be home soon."

David felt like squirming too. He was tired, his long legs felt cramped from sitting for the most of twelve hours, and his shirt was clinging to his back with sweat. One more time he wondered whether he had made a big mistake in coming.

"It will be good for you to connect with your roots," his Mum had said. "*Aachi* will be so happy to see you. She isn't getting any younger, you know. She has longed to see you ever since you were born. Besides, it will be good for you to experience the place where your Dad and I grew up and see for yourself where your family is from. It is part of your heritage" She usually got this way whenever she spoke of Jaffna. Her eyes would get all misty and she would go on about the beautiful palm trees and the simple way of life and the importance of children being brought up with family values. "If not for the war we would still all be there together," she had sighed. "I think this is the best time for you to visit *Aachi*. The situation is fairly stable over there right now, and you are old enough to find your way around. Deepa *mami* said they'll be happy to have you."

David had never been to Sri Lanka, though he had heard a lot about it from his parents. They had migrated to Canada in the early '80s when the civil unrest had begun. David's parents were from Jaffna, the Northern Province which was the home of many of the Tamil minorities in Sri Lanka. Shortly after David was born the political situation in Sri Lanka had gotten more volatile and so his parents had decided not to visit Jaffna till they felt it was safe. David knew about the civil war between the Sinhalese majority and the Tamil minority, in the Tamil rebels' efforts to secure a separate state. Even though David's Dad had returned to Sri Lanka from time to time and his Mum went once when his grandma had been ill, his parents had not felt it was safe for David to go there yet as the political climate was particularly dangerous for young Tamil males who were often suspected to be part of the rebellion.

Growing up in Victoria, David had always felt like a stranger. Attending a private school mostly populated by Anglo students, he looked different from his classmates, he could hardly understand his parents when they spoke in Tamil with each other, and he resembled neither of his parents in appearance. His Dad was about five feet eight and his Mum was a petite five feet, while David towered above both of his parents at a little over six feet. Except for the honey collared eyes that he shared with his mother, he looked so different from his parents that he could have been adopted. And, unlike his parents who were both of a calm disposition, David was always energetic and restless, constantly looking for something new to stimulate him. All through high school he had joined various sport teams in search of a place where he could feel like he belonged. Now, as a freshman in college, he was still searching. He hadn't even decided on a major yet.

His parents had tried their best to teach him Tamil and introduce him to Sri Lankan ways. David found it hard to learn the language, but he enjoyed Sri Lankan food and hoped that one day he would get to go to Sri Lanka. But the reason for his desire to visit Sri Lanka was not necessarily to connect with his "roots." He didn't feel any particular affection for the country. All his life he had heard about his relatives in Jaffna and had seen pictures of people he had never met, but he felt no connection with them. But Sri Lanka seemed like a distant exotic land, shrouded by mystery and danger. And David liked adventures. So when his parents suggested that he should visit his grandma during the holidays, he had jumped at the idea. They had made arrangements for him to stay with his aunt Deepa, with whom his grandma also lived. He would fly to the capital city of Colombo and then catch a bus to Jaffna. His parents had ensured that David would have all the necessary documents and the contact information of people who could assist him if needed.

David's hope for an exciting adventure had evaporated when the reality of being in Sri Lanka set in. The crowded airport swarmed with armed guards and the repeated questioning he received at every check point on the way to town served as constant reminders of the two decades of war that had taken a toll on the country. It didn't matter that David was Canadian. His appearance and his last name signalled that he was Tamil and that meant he needed to be questioned. Colombo was a busy metropolis, crowded with people who did not seem to mind being out in the sweltering heat. David's Dad's friend had accommodated him for the night and dropped him off at the bus station the following afternoon. And before he knew it, he was on his way to Jaffna.

The bus came to a screeching halt and the driver announced, "Jaffna junction."

David picked up his bags and descended the steps, screening the small crowd that had gathered to greet the passengers.

"David, over here," a short stout man waved at him as he elbowed his way to the front. "You are tall!" His bearded face broke into a wide grin, as he embraced David in a tight hug.

"Ranjit *mama*?" David said hesitantly as he was released. He thought he recognised his uncle from his picture, but his uncle seemed a little shorter than David had imagined.

"Ah, you have a nice Canadian accent!" the bearded man laughed heartily. "Yes, I am Ranjit *mama*. Come on, let's get your bags in the taxi. Your *mami* and cousin are anxious to see you." They loaded the bags into the waiting cab and were off. David took in the tall palmera trees and the intricate architecture of the buildings. The colonial influence was evident in the city. There were also many buildings in ruins, reflecting the years of civil war.

"Are you hungry?" Uncle Ranjit asked from the front seat. "Your *mami* is making a very special lunch for you."

"Thank you," David said, not knowing how else to respond. It was strange to be talking to his Mum's brother-in-law. It felt like he should be familiar to him in some way because they were related, but instead David felt that he was talking to a complete stranger—perhaps because he *was* a complete stranger. "Your grandma isn't home today," Uncle Ranjit continued. "She went to a nearby town to visit a friend yesterday. There was a shooting incident there last night, and they have closed off all traffic. She should be able to make it back tomorrow." "Don't worry," he added, seeing the look of shock on David's face, "These things happen here all the time. We are used to it. As long as we take certain precautions, it is quite safe."

The taxi pulled into a narrow driveway and came to a halt in front of a large one-story house. At the front of the house was a covered veranda with tall white columns going all the way up to the roof. There were wicker chairs and several potted plants on the veranda. On either side of the house were many large trees, giving the illusion of being in the middle of the woods.

"*Amma*, they are here!" squealed a little girl as she came running into view. She had on a flowery cotton dress, her hair tied into two pigtails, and she looked about six. "Asha, come here and say hello to David *anna*," said Uncle Ranjit, as he scooped her up into his arms. David set his luggage down and smiled at her. She smiled back shyly and buried her face in her father's shoulder. "Oh, she's shy now, but wait till you get to know her. You won't be able to silence her!" Uncle Ranjit winked at him and led the way into the house, with Asha still clinging to him. "Deepa," he called. "Look who I found at the bus stop."

David took in the spacious living room, also furnished with wicker furniture. There were more potted plants inside and several pictures on the walls. He recognised a picture of himself from when he was ten.

"*Vaango, vaango*," said a beautiful lady who had just entered the room. David looked at his mother's only sister for the first time. She was wearing a light green sari and wore her long dark hair in a single braid. She looked nothing like his mother except for her petite frame. She reached up and kissed David on both his cheeks. "Oh, I forgot you don't speak much Tamil," she said as she released him. She beamed up at him, still cupping his face. "You are a tall young man, aren't you?" David was surprised to see her eyes well up with tears. "Come, you must be tired," she said, regaining her composure. "You can have a quick bath and then we will all have lunch." She took his hand and led him to a room at the end of the hallway, which had been prepared for him. David noticed how open and ventilated the house felt owing to the many large windows that let in the warm sunlight.

The rest of the day went by quickly. David felt a little awkward despite his uncle and aunt's warm hospitality. Aunt Deepa kept serving him several helpings of her delicious cooking and Uncle Ranjit loaned him one of his cotton sarongs which was very comfortable to wear in the hot weather. He discovered that his little cousin was indeed very chatty when she warmed up to people. She kept following him around and asking him to play with her dolls. By six o'clock David was exhausted, and excused himself to bed after pleading jetlag.

As he lay down, he couldn't help feeling disappointed. He had had a long and tiring journey to get here. But he wasn't sure whether it was worth it. He realised that he had been hoping for a feeling of belonging or familiarity with the place where his parents had once lived. But even here he felt like a stranger. He still towered above everyone and he wasn't sure whether it was his eyes, which were lighter than most Sri Lankans' eyes, or the way he dressed, but he had stood out enough for even the guard to notice that he was different from the others. He drifted away into restless sleep.

* * *

David awoke to the sound of a rooster. It took him a moment to realise where he was. It was still dark and the house was quiet. The clock at his bedside glowed 5:00. He felt wide awake. Figuring he might as well get up, he quietly washed up in the bathroom down the hallway and decided to go sit out on the veranda till the others woke up.

He stopped short when he stepped out. He wasn't alone.

David had only seen pictures of his grandmother from when she was much younger. Now at seventy one, he had imagined her to be a frail little old wrinkled lady with dishevelled gray hair. The lady who was sitting at the veranda with a cup of tea was nothing like what he had imagined. She did have gray hair, but it was neatly piled in a low bun. The deep lines on her face, far from making her appear frail and wrinkled, accentuated the aura of strength and wisdom that she exuded.

She lifted her honey collared eyes to meet David's. He was suddenly overwhelmed by a sense of familiarity, as if he was looking into the eyes of his mother. "David," she said in a gentle deep voice as her face broke into a warm smile. She held out her hand. "You are up early. Come, let me see you." Even her voice was strangely familiar. He walked closer and leaned over to embrace her. She smelled like fresh jasmine and sandalwood. She hugged him and kissed him on both cheeks, and held onto his hands as he sat on the wicker chair next to her.

David felt her eyes studying his face closely. "You have your mother's eyes," she stated. She reached up and touched his hair gently. "Is it strange to be here?" she asked, as if reading his mind.

"No, *Aachi*," he said, looking down. Then he hesitated and added, "Yes, a little bit." He looked at the wrinkled soft hand that was holding his. "When did you get back?"

"Around eight last night. They cleared the roads earlier than expected, and I was anxious to see you. But you were fast asleep so I didn't wake you up." She spoke with a British accent, slightly more pronounced than his parents'.

"I have waited a long time to see you," she continued. "I'm glad you came." She sipped her tea. "Would you like some tea?"

"No, thank you," he replied, still surprised by how familiar his grandmother seemed to him.

"David, do you know whom you are named after?" she asked, after a brief silence.

"Yes, I heard grandpa liked that name," he replied.

"Yes, he did. Do you know why?" David shook his head.

"You are named after King David." She set her cup of tea down and turned to look at him. "Your grandpa always wanted a son so that he could name him David, after the man who sought God's own heart. He was moved by David's character and passion for God. But, as you know, we had two girls, and when your mother was little your grandpa used to tell her that she must give him a grandson so he could name him David. But he didn't even live to see her get married." She sighed and looked away at the first signs of dawn on the horizon. "He would have been so happy to see you."

David had heard about the heart attack that had killed his grandpa when he was merely forty five. Apparently he had been playing tennis when it happened.

"You look just like him," his grandma said softly. "Tall, handsome, and a face that reveals a strong will. He was a very adventurous man, always full of energy and active, up to his very last breath."

He looked up to find her smiling at him and, somehow, for the first time, he felt at home.

"I'd like to hear more about him," he said, smiling in return. "And I am glad to finally meet you, *Aachi.*" To his horror he realised his eyes were watering. He hurriedly looked away.

"Welcome home, David," said his grandmother as she leaned over and kissed him softly on his forehead. "I have missed you."

Interview with David

Lily: Hello David. Thank you for taking time to talk about your experiences.

David: No problem, it is my pleasure.

Lily: Can you talk a bit about your experience of growing up in Canada?

David: Sure. It was mostly great, but it was also challenging because I didn't quite fit in anywhere, you know? At home my parents kept living like they were living in Sri Lanka, eating Sri Lankan dishes, always socialising with Sri Lankans, and acting as if I was somehow Sri Lankan. But I'd never been there before I went to visit my grandma. So it was weird to try to live as if I was part of a certain culture when I really knew nothing about it . . . apart from what my parents told me . . . and really didn't feel any affiliation to it as such.

Lily: So you felt Canadian then?

David: Yes . . . and no. I wasn't *totally* Canadian. Even though Canada is quite diverse, white Canadians are still at least subconsciously considered the norm. So I didn't look Canadian in the traditional sense of the term, and I didn't know what it meant to be Canadian because my parents didn't either. Things got a bit easier as I grew up, but I guess I'm what you'd call a third culture kid—neither fully Sri Lankan, nor fully Canadian—whatever that means!

Lily: Well said! How did visiting your grandma help you in your quest for cultural identity?

David: At first I regretted going to Jaffna—it was quite a strange and frightening experience, really. But meeting grandma was the best thing! Somehow she understood what I was feeling—and she was *so* familiar to me even though I'd never met her before that visit. It was weird—in a good way! Growing up in Canada, I didn't consider myself to be necessarily connected to my extended family in an intimate way. I saw myself as an individual who can make my own decisions and carve my own path to my destiny without being influenced by the larger community. But meeting my grandma . . . somehow made me feel more *whole* than ever before. As I talked to her and got to know a bit about where my parents came from—where I came from, I guess—it became easier to embrace my mixed unique cultural identity. I didn't feel more Sri Lankan by just being there and getting to know grandma, but I felt more *me*.

Lily: Do you think that is a typical experience that children of migrant parents would have should they choose to visit their parents' country of origin?

David: I don't know. I don't think it's something formulaic. In my case I think I needed to understand and experience *both* cultures which contributed to my unique third culture in order to feel comfortable in it. I don't think it's helpful to deny either culture—somehow they are both part of me. But that doesn't mean I have to fit neatly into one or the other—I can be both, and neither!

Lily: There's this concept of individualistic and collectivistic cultures prevalent in intercultural communication literature. I would say that the mainstream culture in Canada is more oriented toward individualism and the mainstream Sri Lankan culture is oriented to collectivism. Based on your own negotiation of cultural identity, can you comment on where you stand in this continuum of individualism to collectivism?

David: Had you asked me this question prior to my visit to Jaffna, I would have probably answered that I am inclined to individualism. Having experienced a sense of identity and connection once meeting my grandma, however, I wonder whether there is more collectivist in me than I realised!

Lily: Thank you, David. Your thoughts certainly give the readers something to mull over.

Story 4: Adaptation

It was nearly three o'clock when Alejandro got off at the Stathfield station. He followed the crowd down the ramp to the underground lobby where several monitors were displaying the outbound trains. He scanned the monitors for a familiar station. It took him a while to see what he was looking for. Eastwood. The monitor showed that the next train to Eastwood was leaving in 8 minutes from platform 6. Looking around, Alejandro located the ramp up to platform 6 and started ascending toward the platform.

He was hungry, as he had not had lunch. He had been going from one place to another all day, running errands and getting things organised. Alejandro knew that moving to a new country would be challenging. But he had forgotten how challenging it could be. He had been in Sydney for nearly two months now, and he was still very disoriented and unsettled. He found it hard to remember the places, the train routes, and the landmarks. It was hard not to miss his friends in New York. It was even harder not to miss Stella.

Alejandro had lived in New York most of his life. His parents had migrated to New York from Mexico City when Alejandro was two. He hardly remembered Mexico because he had only been back once when he was about ten. Though there had been many opportunities to visit Mexico since that time, Alejandro had simply chosen not to. New York was where he felt at home. He loved the constant liveliness of the city and the endless food establishments around every corner. As the only son of a wealthy businessman, Alejandro received every comfort that his parents could afford. He attended the top schools and earned the top grades in every class. He was successful in whatever he chose to do. By the time he had finished high school he had offers from just about every Ivy-league university in the country. But he had chosen to stay in New York for college because he couldn't bear to part with the city—and with Stella.

Just as New York was a part of him, so was Stella. He had known Stella for most of his life, as she and her family lived right next door to Alejandro's family. They attended the same schools, did homework together, played on the streets, and, when they grew up, had realised that they could not possibly have a romantic relationship with anybody else than with each other. They had made all kinds of plans about what they would do once they finished college and got married. Stella was studying to be a veterinarian, so she had several years of college ahead. But that worked out well with Alejandro's plans to become a lawyer. He wanted to have enough time to establish a practice after finishing law school, before they would get married. Both sets of parents were delighted with these plans, as they knew one another very well and fully approved of Alejandro and Stella's relationship.

Everything had gone well until Alejandro failed his bar exam. He could hardly believe his eyes as he stared at the sheet of paper which informed him of his results. He had walked into his room, closed the door, and refrained from speaking to anyone for a whole day. He couldn't even speak to Stella. He had no idea what had happened. He knew he was a bit preoccupied when he was studying, but he was very confident that he would pass with top grades as he had always done—perhaps he was too confident. He felt like his whole world had come crashing down. He had never failed at anything before. When Stella had come knocking on his door the following morning, he barely made eye contact with her and asked her to give him some time to process things. Alejandro had always been a systematic man, planning ahead for things and following the plan to the letter. But now all that he had planned had come to a screeching halt. He knew he could take the bar again, he knew he could even do something completely different if he wanted to, but he couldn't entertain any of these thoughts. He couldn't get past the fact that he had failed at something. And now he was out of sync with Stella, who was successfully completing each year of her studies. They were supposed to finish their separate endeavours together, before their marriage. Now he had fallen behind.

"The train on platform 6 goes to Hornsby," announced the mechanical voice on the intercom.

Alejandro got on board and found a seat on the top deck. He was glad he would be back at his apartment within half an hour. He was looking forward to the leftover Chinese food in the fridge. Stella loved Chinese food, he recalled with sadness.

The months that followed Alejandro's failing of the bar exam brought a strain on his relationship with Stella. He found himself withdrawing from her, secluded in his thoughts of inadequacy, and she started becoming impatient with him. It all came to a breaking point when Alejandro had forgotten the anniversary of their first real date. Stella had shown up at his door at eight o'clock in the evening, wearing her favourite magenta dress. She had clearly been waiting for him to "surprise" her with dinner plans, as he usually did on their anniversary. She had just one sentence to say, but that sentence left a long lasting scar in him: "You can't be in a relationship with me till you know who you are, Alejandro." And she had walked out.

Alejandro had spent the next several days trying to persuade her to change her mind, to explain that he had been going through a "phase" and that he was ready to get back into the swing of things. But Stella did not want to reconsider her decision. She said that perhaps they had stuck to each other for so long that they had missed other opportunities they could've had and that perhaps it was time to explore those opportunities. It was too late before Alejandro realised that he had taken her for granted. He was heartbroken.

When his uncle suggested that Alejandro should move to Sydney to help him with his new business, Alejandro accepted the offer. He just wanted to get away from all the broken dreams. To go somewhere far, for a fresh start.

The train came to a halt at Eastwood and Alejandro stepped out. It had been a hard two months in Sydney. Even though Alejandro's uncle had been very helpful in getting him set up with an apartment and a job, Alejandro found the emptiness in his heart almost unbearable. It was like walking alone in the midst of a crowd. Everywhere he looked, he saw people talking to friends, speaking into their mobile phones, and hurrying about on some busy errand. But none of them knew him. He had bought a mobile phone, but it had only rung once in the past three days and that was because his uncle was calling to check whether Alejandro had sent the fax he was supposed to. He remembered his cell phone in New York, which was full of numbers of friends with whom he spoke daily. Back then hardly fifteen minutes went by after finishing one call before he would have to answer another. It was one more reminder to Alejandro that moving to a new place is a very lonely venture. He had met a few people, his neighbour Anita and her husband Pete, for example, but it was hard to really connect with people in a short time. As Alejandro had lived in New York for so long, he had not realised that making friends takes time and work. He couldn't remember the last time he felt new or out of place.

As he opened the door to his barely furnished apartment, Alejandro wondered for the tenth time (that day) why he had moved to Sydney. It had seemed like a good idea to get away from everything. But making a new start seemed even harder. The hardest part was to pretend that all was well and make polite conversations with new people you meet, all the while hurting on the inside and wishing somebody knew you—wishing you could be just yourself with somebody.

As he opened the fridge to grab the leftover Chinese food, he heard a knock on the door. A cheerful face with a big grin peered at him as he opened the door. It was his neighbour, Anita.

"Hi Alejandro. How're you going?" she said, and without waiting for an answer, proceeded to say, "We're having a barbi later this evening, and I was wondering whether you'd like to come along. Pete has invited some of his mates from work too. I thought you may like to join us?"

"Yeah, sure," said Alejandro. "Thanks."

Having showered and dressed, Alejandro headed over to Anita and Pete's that evening, not looking forward to yet another evening where he would have to make polite conversations with nameless strangers. But he had decided to go anyway because he had come to the realisation in the past month that meeting new people was the only way to make friends in a place where you know nobody.

Pete and Anita had set up the grill in their backyard, and a tantalising aroma of searing steak greeted Alejandro as he joined the small crowd that had gathered.

"Hey Alejandro," Pete greeted him enthusiastically. "Glad you could come. Come over here and meet some of my mates." He introduced Alejandro to four or five people, all of whom smiled and exchanged pleasantries.

"Hey you guys, your place is so hard to find!" called a new comer who had just walked in. She was petite with long curly brown hair. She wore a wide grin as she hugged Anita. "I finally made it!"

"Alejandro, this is my colleague Dina. She is quite new to Sydney too. She just moved here a couple of months ago, from Canada."

Alejandro shook hands with Dina. "I'm glad to meet someone from North America," he said. Dina smiled back. "You're American, eh? Where're you from?"

"New York"

"Really? I studied at NYU! I loved it there," she grinned. "How do you like Sydney?"

"Well . . . ," said Alejandro, not knowing what to say. How to express how he was feeling? How to say that he wished somebody knew him in this big city full of people or that just for one day he would not have to meet yet another new person or that just for one day he wished he would not miss New York? How could he possibly express that every day he felt like the only stranger in a sea of people who all inexplicably seem to know one another?

"It's hard being in a new place, isn't it?" Dina said, as if reading his mind. "The first month I was here I was so tired of meeting new people all the time and getting lost at different train stations! But now things are slowly getting better." She smiled. "Have you met Brian yet? He's American too."

Brian turned out to be another one of Pete's colleagues, and he too had recently moved to Sydney from America. Alejandro spent an extraordinarily good time talking to Dina and Brian about things he missed from home, things he found strange in Sydney, and things he wished somebody had told him before he moved across the world! He suddenly realised he wasn't the only one feeling alone in a big city. There were at least two others. Two more numbers were added to Alejandro's mobile phone that night.

* * *

"Alejandro, could you please bring in the mushrooms, honey? The meat is getting cold," called Angela from the kitchen.

Alejandro quickly scooped up the mushrooms from the outdoor barbeque and put them in a dish. He knew that tone in his wife's voice—it meant "hurry up, our guests are waiting!" He picked up the dish of grilled mushrooms and headed into the crowded dining room.

It was their annual pre-Christmas party, and the house was full of friends and guests. Angela was scurrying around making sure everyone was comfortable and well supplied with munchies and drinks.

"Ah, there you are, honey. Thank you for these," she smiled, and reached up to kiss him as she retrieved the dish from his hands.

Alejandro kissed her back and smiled into the beautiful face of his wife of two years. "You've outdone yourself with this party, love. Looks like everyone's having a great time," he said.

"Hey Alejandro, I'd like you to meet Adrian," called Pete, as he walked over with a tall young man with blonde hair. "Adrian just moved to Sydney from Germany."

"Hello Adrian," said Alejandro, and shook hands with him. "How are you settling in?"

"Oh, well. OK, I suppose," Adrian responded, smiling hesitantly. Suddenly Alejandro recalled a lonely afternoon in Eastwood when he had returned to his apartment, looking forward to some leftover Chinese food.

"It gets easier, Adrian," he smiled and patted Adrian's shoulder. "Come over and meet my friends. You've met Pete and Anita, obviously. There's Angela, my wife, the beautiful lady who's running around filling people's drinks" he grinned, "and there's Gary, and . . . "

Interview with Alejandro

Lily: Hello Alejandro. I hope you don't mind talking a bit about your experience moving to a new country.

Alejandro: Not at all. Thank you for the opportunity. Well, as you know I grew up in New York as an immigrant kid and went through all the identity crisis experiences associated with that! I also had many friends from all over the world, and so I didn't think it would be hard to move to Australia. I figured it would take me a couple of months to fully acclimate.

Lily: Were you mistaken?

Alejandro: Very much so! Granted, I moved under extreme emotional stress, having just broken up with my steady girlfriend and everything else that was going on. But I don't think that is a unique thing—I think many migrants move under extreme emotional stress. Even if the reason for their move isn't something dramatic like fleeing from persecution or, like in my case, fleeing from broken dreams, moving to another country is a very emotional affair because you're leaving behind everything that's familiar to you and starting fresh in a new place. Even though that may sound appealing if you're leaving behind hard circumstances, starting "fresh" means not knowing anyone, and worse—not being known by anyone. You're just a stranger in a crowd—nobody knows what you've done or where you've been—it feels like you've lost all your worth and value in one fell swoop.

Lily: Surely, your value doesn't diminish when you move to a new country?

Alejandro: In a way it does—at least at first. Think about it—a person's social value is based on what other people think of him and how much they trust him, like him, seek him, etc. If nobody knows anything about him, he has no social value apart from the fact that he is a breathing alive human being. He has to *build* social value by making friends, making himself known to people, proving he can be trusted, sharing his past experiences, and building relationships. That takes work! And it is hard to put effort into that when you're hurting from whatever emotional baggage you carried with you from your old country.

Lily: What you're referring to is different from *cultural* adaptation that's extensively discussed in textbooks, isn't it?

Alejandro: Yes. It is related to adapting to a new culture, yes, but I'm talking about the process of building social value. And yes, in order to build social value by building relationships, you have to learn the ways of socialisation in the new culture. That's why you often find migrants sticking to their own cultural groups because the process of building social value is easier if you don't have to first learn how to socialise. For example, in the migrant Mexican-American community which my parents associate with in New York, you had great social value if you had affluence or had kids who were high academic performers. Knowing that, I know that regardless of where I go in the world if I find a migrant Mexican-American community I will have certain social value by merely making my academic credentials and family affiliation known. But I wouldn't know the appropriate social currency amongst local Australians unless I stick around, observe, and do the hard work necessary to build relationships. If I am unwilling to do that then it is easier to just stick to the Mexican-American community.

Lily: And is that so wrong?

Alejandro: Yes, in a way it is. Well, let me rephrase. It's not *wrong*, but it is unhelpful. What's the point of going to a new country if you never quite experience it? If you only associate with your own group of people then you not only miss out on what the country has to offer but also debilitate your ability to be a fully functioning member of that society. Your social skills will be limited to only your group of people and you would in turn deprive the members of the host country from learning from your experiences and cultural perspective.

Lily: That is a very idealistic stance, and I fully agree. But is it practical?

Alejandro: Of course it is. I am proof that it can be done! Granted, I knew the language so it was easier for me than for someone who may have to learn the language as well. But unless you make the effort to build relationships with the local people in a new country you'll never fully acclimate, in my opinion, set themselves up to be stagnant. Think about it, if a family migrates to a new country, and decides to associate only with other migrants from their country, then they start bringing up their children in the ways of their old country.

Meanwhile, their children grow up a bit confused, neither here nor there, and to make things worse they grow up with an unrealistic picture of the country from which their parents come because the parents carry on as if time has stood still in their old country and enforce traditions and values that may no longer be relevant in their old country because time has moved on and things have changed in their absence.

Lily: That's a sobering consequence of being a parochial migrant. Do you have any thoughts on how members of the host culture can facilitate the cultural transition of new immigrants?

Alejandro: Sure, I do. If my neighbours Pete and Anita hadn't taken the initiative to invite me over and befriend me, I would've been quite lonely for a long time. But they were kind, and I appreciate their thoughtfulness even to this day. I think members of the host culture need to remember that new migrants may not always take the initiative in building friendships because they are often unfamiliar with the social norms, unaware of the expectations of the local culture, and disoriented in the new environment. Also, many of them could even be in emotional pain or suffering from mild depression due to missing their home country or missing people they've left behind. These are not ideal conditions for braving new friendships. Hence the members of the host culture are in a better position to reach out in friendship to new immigrants than the other way around. Now that I'm comfortably "Australian," I try to remember this when I meet new immigrants and try to extend them friendship—just as Peter and Anita did to me.

Lily: Thank you for sharing your thoughts, Alejandro.

Story 5: Promise

Allahu akbar. . . . Allahu akbar. . . .

Meera woke up with a start. She felt disoriented and wondered where she was and what had woken her. Then the droning of the 5AM prayer call that rang through town reminded her where she was. She kicked her sheets away and checked to see whether the ceiling fan was still on. It was so hot. Her hair was sticking to her forehead which was wet with perspiration. Even though the sun hadn't even risen yet, it was already promising to be a typical sweltering hot day in Male'. She sat up and contemplated whether she should try going back to sleep. She was still getting used to hearing the prayer call on the loud speakers, five times a day. The early morning one always woke her up and she usually could not fall back to sleep. She decided to get up and get started with her day. She had to be at work in a couple of hours anyway.

She gathered some fresh clothes and headed for the bathroom. As she turned on the tap and caught a handful of water, she was once again startled by how cold the water felt even though it was so hot outside. There were no hot water taps in the Maldives. They were not necessary. Everyone showered in cold water because it was a refreshing reprieve from the heat. But the first step into the icy cold shower was always a shock to the system. Meera let her mind wander to what she had to accomplish that day at work. She had three classes, a staff meeting, and some papers to correct. She stepped out of the shower, dried herself, got dressed, and headed for the small kitchen.

It was more like a narrow closet than a kitchen. As space was a priced commodity in Male', Meera was thankful to have found a little apartment of her own, even though it was just a room with an attached bathroom and the tiny 'kitchen.' It was sufficient for her needs. She turned on the light, filled the kettle with water, lit the gas stove, and put the kettle down on it. She was still getting used to having to have the lights on even during the day because of the lack of sufficient windows in the small box-like buildings in Male'. She sat down at the small table in her kitchen and stretched her legs. Her legs almost touched the opposite wall. This cramped space was a far cry from what she was used to.

Meera had grown up in America, even though her parents were originally from India. Being the only daughter of parents who were both doctors, she had attended the best schools and had access to every comfort imaginable. Her one regret in life was that she did not have a sibling with whom to share her experiences. She envied her friends who had sisters with whom they could share clothes and brothers with whom they could argue.

It was in her second semester at college that she had met Aisha. Aisha was an international student from the Maldives. As they were both majoring in Chemistry, they had several classes together and the more time they spent with each other the more they enjoyed each other's company. Aisha had a carefree disposition, always laughing and not taking herself too seriously. Meera enjoyed listening to Aisha talk about how she missed her family who lived in Male', the capital island. Every time she spoke of her home her eyes would shine with a passion and love that intrigued Meera. Meera had never been to India. Growing up in a bicultural family, she never felt that she completely belonged anywhere. She had never felt the kind of passion for a country or home that Aisha seemed to feel for the Maldives. Aisha showed her many pictures of the beautiful white beaches and crystal clear blue waters of the Maldive Islands.

When Aisha's lease expired and Meera happened to be looking for a roommate at that time, it was an easy decision for them to start sharing a small two bedroom apartment near campus. Meera invited Aisha to visit her family over the holidays, and Aisha enjoyed Meera's mother's Indian cooking which was similar to what she was used to eating in the Maldives. "You must come and visit me in Male'," Aisha would say. "You'll love it." Even though they had tried to plan a trip to the Maldives during the holidays a couple of times, their plans had fallen through due to one reason or another. One time Aisha's mother had gotten sick and it was just not a good time to take a friend back with her, and another time when they had planned a summer trip to the Maldives, Meera had received an internship that she had really wanted and so she had chosen to take that instead. But they kept talking about a trip to the Maldives, even if it had to be after their graduation.

Their friendship grew over the years. Their bond was made stronger by some trying experiences through which they supported each other, such as the time when Aisha's boyfriend broke up with her and Meera sat up with her all night as she cried, or when Meera slipped on ice and fractured her ankle and Aisha waited on her hand and foot to make sure she was comfortable. They argued with each other from time to time too, but it only increased their level of comfort with each other. Meera was beginning to feel like she finally had the sister that she had always wanted.

Their senior year in college came all too soon and it was time to start thinking about career options. As Aisha was on a government scholarship, she already knew she would return to the Maldives and teach, to fulfil her contract. Meera, however, had no idea what she wanted to do. Her parents had suggested that she apply for graduate schools, but she felt like she needed to take some time off before going back to school.

It was Aisha who came up with a solution. "I have a great idea!" she had said, grinning from ear to ear with excitement. "Why don't you come to Male' with me and teach there for one year? We are always looking for teachers, and I'm sure my cousin can put in a good word for you. He works at MEC." Meera knew that MEC stood for Male' Educational Centre, the only high school in Male'. "It will be a good experience for you and we will get to be together for one more year! I can show you all my favourite places—it'd be great!" Aisha's enthusiasm was infectious. Meera had always wanted to travel, and this would be a good opportunity, she thought, because she would have a native person to show her around and help her get used to the local customs. She discussed the idea with her parents, and, after ensuring that Meera would be safe and only a one hour flight away from their relatives in India, her parents agreed that it was a good plan.

They spent the rest of their senior year making plans for their trip and day dreaming about all the fun things they would do together. "On the weekends we should take the boat to *Kudabandos*," Aisha would say. "My cousins and I used to go there almost every weekend and just play in the water. It's one of my favourite islands." Meera could hardly wait to see all the beautiful places that Aisha had described. She had received a position as an English teacher (they did not have any vacancies in Chemistry at that time, as they had hired Aisha to teach Chemistry) at MEC and she was looking forward to being in the place that was so dear to Aisha. "Promise me you won't change your mind about our plan," Aisha had said one day, only half in jest. "I don't want to get all excited and then feel disappointed if you meet a handsome man before we graduate and decide to marry him and stay in America!" "I promise," Meera had replied. "Besides, I don't want to miss out on meeting all those handsome Maldivian men you keep raving about!"

She was supposed to have been with Aisha when the accident happened. But she had left her notes at home. As they were already running late for class, she had urged Aisha to go ahead without her while she ran back home to grab the notes. She even heard the screeching of tires from faraway when she was rushing into her apartment, but thought nothing of it as she had sprinted to her room to grab her notes and dashed out without pausing for breath. She had taken a shortcut to class and had made it just in time as the teacher was walking in. It was strange that Aisha wasn't already in her usual seat, but it wasn't till fifteen minutes into class that Meera really started to worry about why her friend was missing. By the time the class was over there were already murmurings in the hallways about a bad accident that had happened just outside campus and that a student was killed instantly. The driver, who was already driving ten miles above the speed limit, had accidentally spilled coffee on himself and lost control of the car for a moment, just as a student was crossing the street. The campus police had identified the victim from the ID in her backpack.

Meera couldn't quite recall the details of the events that transpired after that. As Aisha had listed Meera as her emergency contact, she was one of the first to know. Everything happened in a blurry haze, from making arrangements to have Aisha's body sent back to her family and speaking to her mother on the phone. She had met Aisha's mother once when she had come to visit Aisha for a holiday. It was heart wrenching to hear the cries of a mother who could not understand why her daughter had suddenly been taken away. Meera's parents took care of most of the logistics.

Meera could not remember how she managed to finish her final exams and graduate from college, in the month that followed. She could not bear to live in the same apartment that no longer had Aisha in it, so she moved in with her parents who lived a couple of hours away from the campus. There were days when she thought her grief would consume her. She kept thinking about all the dreams that she and Aisha had had about the time they would spend in the Maldives. She kept remembering the smiling face of her dear friend, whose life had been snatched away in a meaningless act of irresponsibility. Her parents tried to comfort her as best as they could, but the grief was hers alone to bear.

As her graduation day had drawn near, there was a new decision to be faced. She was supposed to begin teaching in the Maldives the following month. But now everything had changed. She no longer had her friend with whom to share the adventure. There was no longer even a reason to go to the Maldives, as the main purpose of the trip was to spend time with Aisha in her country and experience everything that was dear to her. Meera's parents advised her that she should decline the offer from MEC and stay close to home. If she still wanted to travel, she could always visit her relatives in India for a while, to take her mind off things. It all made sense to her. But she had a promise to keep. She had promised Aisha that she would go to the Maldives. And, Meera felt, perhaps this was the best time to do it. She missed her friend so much that nothing in her present surroundings seemed to bring comfort. Perhaps if she went to the Maldives and walked on the streets where her friend had once walked, it would bring her comfort. Despite her parents' reluctance, Meera had decided to proceed with her plan to go to the Maldives to teach at MEC, just as she would have done if Aisha were alive.

The whistle of the kettle brought her back to the present. She got up to make herself a cup of tea. Even though the weather was hot, drinking black tea (or *kalu sai* as the Maldivians called it) with breakfast was common in the Maldives. Meera found that it had a strange calming effect on her, like preparation for the day ahead. A glance at the clock told her that she should start heading for work if she wanted to get there a little early as she had planned. She slipped on her sandals, grabbed her bag which was stuffed with books and papers, and headed out the door into the warm sunlit morning.

She was always amazed by how many cyclists there were on the road. The school was only a ten minute walk from her apartment (pretty much anything was a ten to fifteen minute walk away on the small island of Male'), so she had not purchased a bike like most other people in Male'. She sighed with resignation as a young man on a bicycle whistled at her as he rode past. It had been a hard five months for her. She had never imagined all the challenges she would face in the Maldives, from getting used to dressing in long skirts and dresses even though it was very hot outside, to eating fish for pretty much every meal, to ignoring suggestive comments from men who pass her on the streets. Apparently those comments were a form of flattery, according to the teenage daughter of her landlady. It was hard to get things done the way she was used to doing things in America. She did enjoy teaching, and she knew they had a shortage of teachers at MEC, but she wasn't sure whether all the trouble she was going through was worth it. Even though she had visited Aisha's family from time to time, without Aisha's presence she felt like a stranger in their midst. It was also hard to communicate with Aisha's mother as she did not speak much English. Meera felt quite alone in the strange land, alone without her friend who had promised to show her around. More than once she had wondered why she should not resign and go back home. Her parents would have been only too happy to have her back. But for some reason she had stayed on, and five months had flown by. She only had a few more months to complete her contract at MEC.

She walked into the building where her office was and stopped by the mailboxes. There were more papers from her students.

"Excuse me Miss. Srinivasan, may I please speak with you?"

She turned around to see Adnan, one of her students. "Hello Adnan," she said as she scooped up the papers from her mailbox. "What can I do for you?"

"I was wondering whether you could help me with something," he said hesitantly. "You are from America, no?"

"Yes," she replied, as she walked with him down the hallway toward her office. "Why do you ask?"

"I am thinking of applying to some of the American universities. But my parents are worried because they have seen bad (he pronounced it as *bade*) things in the movies like people doing drugs and gangs and they are worried that it might be dangerous for me to go there. I tell them that it was only in the movies, but they have never been outside of the Maldives, so they are not believing. But since you are from America, I think maybe you could speak to them and explain that it is very safe. I mean, who's going to shoot me, right?" He grinned.

Probably no one, she thought. *But you could get killed crossing the street two blocks from campus by a guy drinking coffee.* She looked up at the eager young face, full of hope for the future. It was students like Adnan that Aisha had wanted to come back and teach. She had had so much hope for her country. She had wanted to help her people. Meera remembered the smiling, carefree face of her friend. She imagined how excited Aisha must have been, just like Adnan was, when she had first decided to go to America to study. She imagined what Aisha would tell him, had he asked her the same question.

"Well," she smiled at him. "I'll be happy to talk to your parents. I'm glad you wish to continue your studies. They must be very proud of you. If you need any help with your university applications, please come and see me."

"Thank you so much!" he beamed. He looked down for a minute and then added, almost shyly, "I also want to thank you for coming here to teach us. My English has improved a lot since last term. See you in class, Miss." With one final wave, he headed off.

Meera watched him go and felt a strange sense of lightness come upon her. It was as if she had been carrying many bags of books on her back all this time and someone had just taken a few of them off. She had come to the Maldives hoping to connect with the memories of her friend. But she realised that what she was actually doing was teaching and helping the young people in Male', just as Aisha had one day hoped to do. Perhaps that's why she had stayed.

She sat down at her desk, picked up the first paper at the top of the pile, and started reading. *The purpose of my essay was to write about my had experience this holiday...* She smiled and picked up her pen to start correcting. *The purpose of my essay* is *to write about* the *experience I had . . .*

Interview with Meera

Lily: Hello Meera. Can you describe your experience of going to the Maldives and finding your place there?

Meera: It was certainly a challenging experience. I went there under great emotional stress, so it compounded the experience of adjusting to a new culture, which is a big challenge by itself even under the best of circumstances. Everything was so new, different, and everyone treated me differently.

Lily: How so?

Meera: I assumed I wouldn't stand out in Male' because my appearance is similar to that of the Maldivians, but somehow everyone knew I was a "foreigner." It was also a shock to be whistled at on the streets or constantly hear comments from men when I walked around because I wasn't used to such behaviour. Like I said, everything was different.

Lily: Didn't this difference in Maldivian culture affect your friendship with Aisha?

Meera: Not entirely. Yes, perhaps at first it took us a while to get to know each other. But Aisha was so easy going—as are most Maldivians—and it was easy to spend time with her and talk to her. Even though the cultural differences were obvious at first, once we got to know each other I forgot that she is actually from a different country. To me she was just my friend Aisha.

Lily: Did it help that she was similar to you in appearance—given both of you are originally from the Indian subcontinent?

Meera: No, I don't think that had anything to do with it. Even though my parents are Indian, I was born and raised in America, so I'm more "white" than anything else. In fact when I see brown people I notice that they are different but when I hang out with my white friends I see myself as one of them.

Lily: That's an interesting observation. So do you think that your cultural identity is the reason why you stood out as a foreigner in the Maldives even though in physical appearance you resemble the Maldivians?

Meera: Maybe. I never thought about it that way.

Lily: How did being in the Maldives help you eventually overcome your grief over Aisha's tragic death?

Meera: Initially I thought being there would somehow help me feel closer to her. But I was wrong. I had never felt more alone than in those first few months in Male'. But then, as I began to get to know the students, I somehow saw her in many of them. They are so full of optimism, full of hope for the future. Many of them had never been outside of the Maldives and they had such big dreams about going abroad to study and experiencing other parts of the world! Aisha was like that. She knew she had been given a unique opportunity to study abroad and she embraced that opportunity with great enthusiasm. She wasn't cynical like me. As I was teaching the students I felt like I was doing something worthwhile with my life—and my grief lightened every day.

Lily: Do you think the fact that you were in a different cultural environment contributed to this process in some way?

Meera: I don't think that's a general rule. I think grief is such that it makes you focus exclusively on yourself, your pain, and the reason for your pain. It distracts you from other people and the responsibilities you have toward them. But when you start focusing on how you can contribute to helping others or enhancing their lives in some way, then grief slowly recedes to the background. But in my case I needed to be outside of my country to recognise this. While I was in America, I only saw things from one perspective. I took for granted my lifestyle, standard of living, social norms, values, beliefs. . . . I knew there were alternative worldviews, but I hadn't experienced any first hand. But when I went to the Maldives I got to see my own country from a different perspective and appreciate the privileges I'd had as well as the delights I had missed by only knowing one corner of the world. My students helped me get a glimpse of this different perspective, and I helped them glimpse my take of the world. We enriched one another's understanding in general. And that was rewarding—and it was healing. I don't think a person has to be in a different cultural environment in order to recognise their place in the world, but in my case I had to.

Lily: Having lived in a couple of countries and encountered a few cultural perspectives, what attitudes and or behaviours would you say served you well in your intercultural interactions?

Meera: I think it is important to recognise that just because someone looks different to you or has had completely different experiences to you, that doesn't mean you cannot relate to that person. I think that's the place to start when interacting with someone from a different culture. I also believe people from other cultures and even people within my own culture who look different from me have valuable insight to offer me because their experiences are different and therefore they see the world from a different perspective. I may not agree with everyone's perspective, but I like finding out about them anyway—so that I can try to understand . . . more. This is the attitude I bring to any conversation with someone who is different from me, and so far it has served me well.

Lily: Thank you for sharing your insight, Meera.

* * *

REFERENCES

Ajzen, I., & Fishbein, M. (1980) *Understanding attitudes and predicting social behavior.* NJ: Prentice-Hall.

Allard, T. (2010). Boat people trade 'out of control.' *Sydney Morning Herald,* April 9.

Allport, G. W. (1954). *The nature of prejudice.* New York, NY: Macmillan.

Amir, Y. (1969). Contact hypothesis in ethnic relations. *Psychological Bulletin, 71,* 319-341.

Anderson, J. A. (1996). *Communication theory: Epistemological foundations.* New York, NY: The Guilford Press.

Anderson, P. A., Hetcht, M. L., Hoobler, G. D., & Smallwood, M. (2002). Nonverbal communication across cultures. In W. B. Gudykunst & B. Mody (Eds.), *Handbook of international and intercultural communication* (pp. 89-106). Thousand Oaks, CA: Sage.

Arasaratnam, L. A. (2003). Competing cultural voices: An ethnographic study of international students in American graduate education. Paper presented at the annual convention of the *National Communication Association,* Miami, FL.

Arasaratnam, L. A. (2004). Sensation seeking as predictor of social initiative in intercultural interactions. *Journal of Intercultural Communication Research, 33,* 215-222.

Arasaratnam, L. A. (2005). Sensation seeking and international students' satisfaction of experiences in the United States. *Journal of Intercultural Communication Research, 34,* 184-194.

Arasaratnam, L. A. (2006). Further testing of a new model of intercultural communication competence. *Communication Research Reports, 23,* 93-99.

Arasaratnam, L. A. (2007). Empirical research in intercultural communication competence: A review and recommendation. *Australian Journal of Communication, 34,* 105-117.

Arasaratnam, L. A. (2008). Acculturation process of Sri Lankan Tamil immigrants in Sydney: An ethnographic analysis using the Bidirectional model (BDM). *Australian Journal of Communication, 35,* 57 - 68.

Arasaratnam, L. A. (2009). The development of a new instrument of intercultural communication competence. *Journal of Intercultural Communication, 20.*

Arasaratnam, L. A., & Banerjee, S. C. (2007). Ethnocentrism and sensation seeking as variables that influence intercultural contact-seeking behavior: A path analysis. *Communication Research Reports, 24,* 303 - 310.

Arasaratnam, L. A., & Banerjee, S. C. (2009). Sensation seeking and intercultural communication competence: A model test. Paper accepted in the Top-3 panel of the intercultural division of the annual convention of the *International Communication Association,* Chicago, IL.

Arasaratnam, L. A., Banerjee, S. C., & Dembek, K. (2010a). The integrated model of intercultural communication competence (IMICC): Model test. Paper presented at the annual convention of the *International Communication Association,* Singapore.

Arasaratnam, L. A., Banerjee, S. C., & Dembek, K. (2010b). Sensation seeking and intercultural communication competence: Further exploration of a model. Paper presented at the annual convention of the *International Communication Association,* Singapore.

Arasaratnam, L. A., & Doerfel, M. L. (2005). Intercultural communication competence: Identifying key components from multicultural perspectives. *International Journal of Intercultural Relations, 29*, 137-163.

Bennett, J. M. (2009). Cultivating intercultural competence: A process perspective. In D. Deardorff (Ed.), *The SAGE handbook of intercultural competence* (pp. 121-140). Thousand Oaks, CA: Sage.

Bennett, J. M., & Bennett, M. J. (2004). Developing intercultural sensitivity: An integrative approach to global and domestic diversity. In D. Landis, J. M. Bennett, & M. J. Bennett (Eds.), *Handbook of intercultural training* (pp. 147-165). Thousand Oaks, CA: Sage.

Berger, C. R. (1979). Beyond initial interaction: Uncertainty, understanding, and the development of interpersonal relationships. In H. Giles & R. St. Clair (Eds.), *Language and social psychology* (pp. 122-144). Oxford: Blackwell.

Berger, C. R. (1986). Uncertain outcome values in predicted relationships: Uncertainty reduction theory then and now. *Human Communication Research, 13*, 34-38.

Berger, C. R., & Calabrese, R. (1975). Some explorations in initial interactions and beyond: Toward a developmental theory of interpersonal communication. *Human Communication Research, 1*, 99-112.

Berger, P. L., & Luckman, T. (1966). *The social construction of reality: A treatise in the sociology of knowledge.* New York, NY: Doubleday.

Berry, J. W. (1980). Acculturation as varieties of adaptation. In A. Padilla (Ed.), *Acculturation: Theory, models, and findings* (pp. 9-25). Boulder, CO: Westview.

Berry, J. W. (2005). Acculturation: Living successfully in two cultures. *International Journal of Intercultural Relations, 29*, 697-712.

Berry, J. W. (2006). Mutual attitudes among immigrants and ethnocultural groups in Canada. *International Journal of Intercultural Relations, 30*, 719-734.

Berry, J. W. (2008). Globalization and acculturation. *International Journal of Intercultural Relations, 32*, 328-336.

Berry, J. W., Kalin, R., & Taylor, D. M. (1977). *Multiculturalism and ethnic attitudes in Canada.* Ottawa: Ministry of Supply and Services.

Berry, J. W., Kim, U., Power, S., Young, M., & Bujaki, M. (1989). Acculturation attitudes in plural societies. *Applied Psychology, 38*, 185–206.

Bhatia, S. & Ram, A. (2009). Theorizing identity in transnational and diaspora cultures: A critical approach to acculturation. *International Journal of Intercultural Relations, 33*, 140-149.

Bhawuk, D. P. S. (2008). Globalization and indigenous cultures: Homogenization or differentiation? *International Journal of Intercultural Relations, 32*, 305-317.

Birdwhistell, R. (1970). *Kinesics and context.* Philadelphia, PA: University of Pennsylvania Press.

Bloch, B., & Dreher, T. (2009). Resentment and reluctance: Working with everyday diversity and everyday racism in southern Sydney. *Journal of Intercultural Studies, 30*, 193-209.

Blumer, H. (1969). *Symbolic interactionism: Perspective and method.* Eaglewood Cliffs, NJ: Prentice Hall.

Brislin, R. (1979). Increasing the range of concepts in intercultural research: The example of prejudice. In W. Davey (Ed.), *Intercultural theory and practice.* Washington, DC: Society for Intercultural Education, Training and Research.

Bruner, J. (1990). *Acts of meaning.* Cambridge, MA: Harvard University Press.

Burgoon, J. K. (1978). A communication model of personal space violations: Explication and an initial test. *Human Communication Research, 4*, 129-142.

Cai, D. A., & Fink, E. L. (2002). Conflict style differences between individualists and collectivists. *Communication Monographs, 69*, 67-87.

Cheng, C. M., & Chartrand, C. L. (2003). Self-monitoring without awareness: Using mimicry as a nonconscious affiliation strategy. *Journal of Personality and Social Psychology, 85*, 1170-1179.

Chong, H. (2006). Stories of intercultural communication conflict lived and told by sojourners in Korea. *Human Communication, 9*, 83-99.

Chirkov, V. (2009). Critical psychology of acculturation: What do we study and how do we study it, when we investigate acculturation? *International Journal of Intercultural Relations, 33*, 94-105.

Collier, M. J. (1989). Cultural and intercultural communication competence: Current approaches and directions for future research. *International Journal of Intercultural Relations, 13*, 287-302.

Cooper, R. C., & Wood, M. (2002). Redemption, Part 1. In Wright, B., & Glassner, J. *Stargate SG-1*. Sci Fi Channel, USA.

Corr, R. (2010). Boat people: This is what you are "anxious" about. *Crickey*, July 6.

De Lima Nunes, A. V., Lins, S. L. B., Camino, L., & Torres, A. R. R. (2010). Social insertion and racial prejudice: Distance from black people and socio-political variables. *Portuguese Journal of Social Science, 9*, 3-17.

De Wall, F. B. M. (2008). Putting the altruism back into the altruism: The evolution of empathy. *Annual Review of Psychology, 59*, 279 – 300.

Deardorff, D. K. (2006). The identification and assessment of intercultural competence as a student outcome of internationalization at institutions of higher education in the United States. *Journal of Studies in International Education, 10*, 241-266.

Deardorff, D. K. (2009). *The SAGE handbook of intercultural competence*. Thousand Oaks, CA: Sage.

Docety, J., & Jackson, P. L. (2004). The functional architecture of human empathy. *Behavioral and Cognitive Neuroscience Review, 3*, 71-100.

Dunn, K. (2003). Attitudes toward immigrants and immigration: An Australian perspective. Paper presented at *New directions, new settlers, new challenges: Building and enhancing communities symposium*, Wellington, New Zealand.

Eckman, P. (1972). Universals and cultural differences in facial expressions of emotion. In J. Cole (Ed.), *Nebraska symposium on motivation, 1971* (pp. 207–283). Lincoln, NE: University of Nebraska Press.

Esses, V. M., Dovidio, J. F., Jackson, L. M., & Armstrong, T. L. (2001). The immigration dilemma: The role of perceived group competition, ethnic prejudice, and national identity. *Journal of Social Issues, 57*, 389-412.

Everett, M. W., & Palmgreen, P. (1995). Influences of sensation seeking, message sensation value, and program context on effectiveness of anticocaine public service announcements. *Health Communication, 7,*225-250.

Fabrigar, L. R., Petty, R. E., Smith, S. M., & Crites, S. L. Jr. (2006). Understanding knowledge effects on attitude-behavior consistency: The role of relevance, complexity, and amount of knowledge. *Journal of Personality and Social Psychology, 90*, 556-577.

Festinger, L. (1957). *A theory of cognitive dissonance*. Stanford, CA: Stanford University Press.

French, J. R. P., & Raven, B. (1959). The bases of social power. In D. Cartright (Ed.), *Studies in social power*. Ann Arbor, MI: Institute for Social Research.

Geertz, C. (1973). *The interpretation of cultures* (pp. 3-13, 412-453). New York: Basic Books.

Gitlin, T. (1972). Sixteen notes on television and the movement. In G. White & C. Neuman (Eds.), *Literature in revolution* (pp. 335-366). NY: Holt, Rinehart, & Winston.

Gitlin, T. (1980). Media routines and political crises. In T. Gitlin (Ed.), *The whole world is watching* (pp. 249-269). Berkeley: University of California Press.

Gitlin, T. (1982). Prime time ideology: The hegemonic process in television entertainment. In H. Newcomb (Ed.), *Television: The critical view*, 3rd ed, (pp 426-454). NY: Oxford University Press.

Greenberg, J., Pyszczynski, T., & Solomon, S. (1986). The causes and consequences of a need for self-esteem: A terror management theory. In R. F. Baumeister (Ed.), *Public Self and Private Self* (pp. 189-212). New York: Springer-Verlag.

Greenberg, J., Pyszczynski, T., Solomon, S., Rosenblatt, A., Veeder, M., Kirkland, S., & Lyon, D. (1990). Evidence for terror management theory II: The effects of mortality salience on reactions to those who threaten or bolster the cultural worldview. *Journal of Personality and Social Psychology, 58*(2), 308-318.

Greenberg, J., Simon, L., Pyszczynski, T., Solomon, S., & Chatel, D. (1992). Terror management and tolerance: Does mortality salience always intensify negative reactions to others who threaten one's worldview? *Journal of Personality and Social Psychology, 63*(2), 212-220.

Gudykunst, W. B. (1993). Toward a theory of effective interpersonal and intergroup communication: An anxiety/uncertainty management (AUM) perspective. In R. L. Wiseman & J. Koester (Eds.), *Intercultural communication competence* (pp. 33-71). Newbury Park, CA: Sage.

Gudykunst, W. B. (1995). Anxiety/uncertainty management (AUM) theory. In R. L. Wiseman (Ed.), *Intercultural communication theory* (pp. 8 – 58). Thousand Oaks, CA: Sage.

Gudykunst, W. B. (2002). Intercultural communication. In W. B. Gudykunst & B. Mody (Eds.), *Handbook of intercultural and intercultural communication* (pp. 179-182). Thousand Oaks, CA: Sage.

Gudykunst, W. B., & Kim, Y. Y. (2003). *Communicating with strangers: An approach to intercultural communication*. New York, NY: McGraw Hill.

Gudykunst, W. B., & Nishida, T. (2001). Anxiety, uncertainty, and perceived effectiveness of communication across relationships and culture. *International Journal of Intercultural Relations, 25*, 55-72.

Hall, E. T. (1966). *The hidden dimension*. Garden City, NY: Anchor/Doubleday.

Hall, E. T. (1973). *The silent language*. New York, NY: Anchor Books.

Hall, E. T. (1976). *Beyond culture*. Garden city, NY: Doubleday.

Hall, E. T. (2003). Monochronic and polychronic time. In L. A. Samovar and R. E. Porter (Eds.), *Intercultural communication: A reader* (pp. 262-268). Belmont, CA: Wadsworth/Thompson Learning.

Heibert, D. (2003). Attitudes toward immigrants and immigration: A Canadian perspective. Paper presented at *New directions, new settlers, new challenges: Building and enhancing communities symposium*, Wellington, New Zealand.

Herfst, S. L., van Oudenhoven, J. P., & Timmerman, M. E. (2008). Intercultural effectiveness training in three Western immigrant countries: A cross-cultural evaluation of critical incidents. *International Journal of Intercultural Relations, 32,* 67-80.

Hofstede (1980). *Culture's consequences.* Beverly Hills, CA: Sage.

Hofstede, (1984). *Culture's consequences: International differences in work-related values* (pp. 65-231). Newbury Park, CA: Sage.

Hofstede, G. (1991). *Cultures and organizations.* London: McGraw Hill.

Inda, J. X., & Rosaldo, R. (2006). *The anthropology of globalization* (pp. 1-34). Oxford: Blackwell.

Kam, C. D., & Kinder, D. R. (2007). Terror and ethnocentrism: Foundations of American support for the war on terrorism. *The Journal of Politics, 69,* 320-338.

Kaushal, R., & Kwantes, C. T. (2006). The role of culture and personality in choice of conflict management strategy. *International Journal of Intercultural Relations, 30,* 579-603.

Kelley, H. H. (1973). The process of causal attribution. *American Psychologist, 28,* 107-128.

Kim, Y. Y. (1995). Cross-cultural adaptation: An integrative theory. In R. L. Wiseman (Ed.), *Intercultural communication theory* (pp. 170-193). Thousand Oaks, CA: Sage.

Kim, Y. Y. (2008). Interpersonal personhood: Globalization and a way of being. *International Journal of Intercultural Relations, 32,* 359-368.

Kim, Y. Y., & Ruben, B. D. (1988). Intercultural transformation: A systems theory. In *Theories in intercultural communication* (pp. 299-321). Beverly Hills, CA: Sage.

Kitao, S. K., & Kitao, K. (1988). Differences in the kinesic codes of Americans and Japanese. *World Communication, 17,* 83-102.

Knafo, A., Zahn-Waxler, C., Van Hulle, C., Robinson, J. L., & Rhee, S. H. (2008). The developmental origins of a disposition toward empathy: Genetic and environmental contributions. *Emotion, 8,* 737-752.

Knapp, M. L., & Hall, J. A. (2007). *Nonverbal communication in human interaction.* Belmont, CA: Wadsworth/Thompson Learning.

LaGravenese, R. (2007). *Freedom writers* [Motion Picture]. Paramount Pictures, USA.

Lakin, J. R., & Chartrand, T. L. (2003). Using nonconscious behavioral mimicry to create affiliation and rapport. *Psychological Science, 14,* 334-339.

Lee, D. (1994). *The color of fear.* [Documentary]. Stirfry Seminars & Consulting.

Lee, T. L., & Fiske, S. T. (2006). Not an outgroup, not yet an ingroup: Immigrants in the stereotype content model. *International Journal of Intercultural Relations, 30,* 751-768.

Leong, C. H. (2007). Predictive validity of the Multicultural Personality Questionnaire: A longitudinal study on the socio-psychological adaptation of Asian undergraduate who took part in a study-abroad program. *International Journal of Intercultural Relations, 31,* 545-559.

Liberman, K. (1990). Intercultural communication in central Australia. In D. Carabaugh (Ed.), *Cultural communication and intercultural contact.* Hillsdale, NJ: Earlbaum.

Lim, T., & Bowers, J. W. (1991). Facework, solidarity, approbation, and tact. *Human Communication Research, 176,* 415-450.

Liu, S. (2007). Living with others: Mapping the routes to acculturation in a multicultural society. *International Journal for Intercultural Relations, 31,* 761-778.

MacRae, C. N., & Bodenhausen, G. V. (2000). Social cognition: Thinking categorically about others. *Annual Review of Psychology, 51,* 93-120.

Maslow, A. H. (1943). A theory of human motivation. *Psychological Review, 50,* 370-396.

McAllister, L., Whiteford, G., Hill, B., Thomas, N., & Fitzgerald, M. (2006). Reflection in intercultural learning: Examining the international experience through a critical incident approach. *Reflective Practice, 7,* 367-381.

McLuhan, M. (1964). *Understanding the media: The extensions of man.* New York, NY: McGraw Hill.

Mead, G. H. (1934). *Mind, self and society: From the standpoint of a social behaviorist.* Chicago: University of Chicago Press.

Miner, H. (1956). Body rituals among the Nacirema. *American Anthropologist, 58,* 503-507.

Morgan, S. E., & Arasaratnam, L. A. (2003). Intercultural friendships as social excitation: Sensation seeking as a predictor of intercultural friendship seeking behavior. *Journal of Intercultural Communication Research, 32,* 175-186.

Morgan, S. E., Arasaratnam, L. A., Layne, W., & Harrison, T. (2002). Predicting attitudes toward intercultural communication with threat buffer theory: Development and testing of the threat buffer inventory. Paper presented at the annual meeting of the *National Communication Association,* New Orleans, LA.

Narushima, Y. (2010). Liberals split over push to move boat people. *Sydney Morning Herald,* May 20.

Neuliep, J. W., Hintz, S. M., & McCroskey, J. C. (2005). The influence of ethnocentrism in organizational contexts: Perceptions of interviewee and managerial attractiveness, credibility, and effectiveness. *Communication Quarterly, 53,* 41-56.

Neuliep, J. W., & McCroskey, J. C. (1997). The development of a U.S. and generalized ethnocentrism scale. *Communication Research Reports, 40,* 385-398.

Oberg, K. (1960). Culture shock: Adjustment to a new cultural environment. *Practical Anthropology, 7,* 177-182.

Oetzel, J., Dhar, S., & Krischbaum, K. (2007). Intercultural conflict from multilevel perspectives: Trends, possibilities, and future directions. *Journal of Intercultural Communication Research, 36,* 183-204.

O'Keefe, D. J., & Sypher, H. E. (1981). Cognitive complexity measures and the relationship of cognitive complexity to communication. *Human Communication Research, 8,* 72-92.

Palmgreen, P., & Donohew, L. (1994). Researching at-risk populations in a mass media drug abuse prevention campaign. *Drugs & Society, 8,* 29-46.

Palmgreen, P., Donohew, L., Lorch, E. P., Hoyle, R., H., & Stephenson, M. T. (2001). Television campaigns and adolescent marijuana use: Tests of sensation seeking targeting. *American Journal of Public Health, 91,*292-297

Pettigrew, T., & Tropp, L. (2000). Does intergroup contact reduce prejudice? In S. Oskamp (Ed.), *Reducing prejudice and discrimination* (pp. 93–114). Mahwah: Erlbaum.

Pettigrew, T., & Tropp, L. (2006). A meta-analytic test of intergroup contact theory. *Journal of Personality and Social Psychology, 90,* 1-33.

Popper, K. R., & Eccles, J. C. (1977). *Self and its brain.* New York, NY: Springer-Verlag.

Ptaszynski, M., Maciejewski, J., Dybala, P., Rzepka, R., & Araki, K. (2010). CAO: A fully automatic emoticon analysis system based on theory of kinesics. *IEEE Transactions of Affective Computing, 99.*

Rahim, M. A. (1983). A measure of styles of handling interpersonal conflict. *Academy of Management Journal, 26,* 368-376.

Rice, R. E., D'Amra, J., & More, E. (1998). Cross-cultural comparison of organizational media evaluation and choice. *Journal of Communication, 48*, 3-26.

Richardson, M. E., & Smith, S. W. (2007). The influence of high/low context and power distance on choice of communication media: Students' media choice to communicate with professors in Japan and America. *International Journal of Intercultural Relations, 31*, 479-501.

Rindfleisch, A., Burroughs, J. E., & Wong, N. (2008). The safety of objects: Materialism, existential insecurity, and brand connection. *Journal of Consumer Research, 36*, 1-16.

Robinovich, A., Morten, T., & Postmes, T. (2010). Time perspective and attitude-behavior consistency in future-oriented behaviors. *British Journal of Social Psychology, 49*, 69-89.

Robson-Orr, S., & Walker, L. (2008). *Blindsight* [Motion picture]. United States: Robson Entertainment.

Rosenblatt, A., Greenberg, J., Solomon, S., Pyszczynski, T., & Lyon, D. (1989). Evidence for terror management theory I: The effects of mortality salience on reactions to those who violate or uphold cultural values. *Journal of Personality and Social Psychology, 57*(4), 681-690.

Ross, L. (1977). The intuitive psychologist and his shortcomings: Distortions in the attribution process. In L. Berkowitz (Ed.), *Advances in experimental social psychology* (pp. 173-219). New York, NY: Academic Press.

Ross, L., & Nisbett, R. E. (1991). *The person and the situation.* New York, NY: McGraw Hill.

Ruben, B. D. (1976). Assessing communication competency for intercultural adaptation. *Group & Organization Studies, 1*, 334-354.

Ruben, B. D. (1983). A systems-theoretic view. In W. B. Gudykunst (Ed.) *Intercultural communication theory: Current perspectives* (pp. 131-145). Beverly Hills, CA: Sage.

Rudmin, F. (2009). Constructs, measurements, and models of acculturation and acculturative stress. *International Journal of Intercultural Relations, 33*, 106-123.

Salzman, M. B. (2008). Globalization, religious fundamentalism, and the need for meaning. *International Journal of Intercultural Relations, 32*, 318-327.

Samovar, L. A., & Porter, R. E. (2004). *Communication between cultures.* Belmont, CA: Wadsworth/Thompson Learning.

Saro, A. (2008). Stereotypes and cultural memory: Adaptation of Oskar Lut's *Spring* in theatre and film. *TRAMES, 12*, 309-318.

See, Y. H. M, Petty, R. E., & Fabrigar, L. R. (2008). Affective and cognitive meta-bases of attitudes: Unique effects on information interest and persuasion. *Journal of Personality and Social Psychology, 94*, 938-955.

Shteynberg, G., Gelfand, M. J., & Kim, K. (2009). Peering into the "magnum mysterium" of culture: The explanatory power of descriptive norms. *Journal of Cross-Cultural Psychology, 40*, 46-69.

Smith, P. B., Dugan, S., Peterson, M. F., & Leung, K. (1998). Individualism-collectivism and the handling of disagreement: A 23-country study. *International Journal of Intercultural Relations, 22*, 351-367.

Solomon, S., Greenberg, J., & Pyszczynski, T. (1991a). Terror management theory of self-esteem. In C. R. Snyder & D. R. Forsyth (Eds.), *Handbook of Social and Clinical Psychology* (pp. 21-40). New York: Pergamon Press.

Solomon, S., Greenberg, J., & Pyszczynski, T. (1991b). A terror management theory of social behavior: The psychological functions of self-esteem and cultural worldviews.

In M. P. Zanna (Ed.), *Advances in Experimental Social Psychology* (Vol. 24, pp. 93-159). San Diego: Academic Press.

Spitzberg, B. H. (1997). A model of intercultural communication competence. In L. A. Samovar & R. E. Porter (Eds.), *Intercultural communication: A reader* (pp. 379-391). Belmont, CA: Wadsworth.

Spitzberg, B. H., & Chagnon, G. (2009). Conceptualizing intercultural competence. In D. K. Deardorff (Ed.), *The SAGE handbook of intercultural competence* (pp. 2 - 52). Sage Publications.

Spitzberg, B. H., & Cupach, W. R. (1984). *Interpersonal communication competence* (pp. 33-71). Beverly Hills, CA: Sage.

Stephan, W. G., Ybarra, O., & Bachman, G. (1999). Prejudice toward immigrants. *Journal of Applied Social Psychology, 29,* 2221-2237.

Stephan, W. G., Renfro, C. L., Esses, V. M., Stephan, C. W., & Martin, T. (2005). The effects of feeling threatened on attitudes toward immigrants. *International Journal of Intercultural Relations, 29,* 1-19.

Stephan, C. W., & Stephan, W. G. (2000). An integrated threat theory of prejudice. In S. Oskamp (Ed.), *Claremont symposium on applied social psychology* (pp.23–46).Hillsdale, NJ: Erlbaum.

Stephan, C. W., & Stephan, W. G. (2002). Cognition and affect in cross-cultural relations. Intercultural communication. In W. B. Gudykunst & B. Mody (Eds.), *Handbook of intercultural and intercultural communication* (pp. 127-142). Thousand Oaks, CA: Sage.

Stephan, W. G., & Stephan, C. W., & Gudykunst, W. B. (1999). Anxiety in intergroup relations: A comparison of anxiety/uncertainty management theory and integrated threat theory. *International Journal of Intercultural Relations, 23,* 613-628.

Stephan, W. G., Ybarra, O., Martinez, C. M., Schwarzwald, J., & Tur-Kaspa, M. (1998). Prejudice toward immigrants to Spain and Israel: An integrated threat analysis. *Journal of Cross-Cultural Psychology, 29,* 559 – 577.

Sumner, W. G. (1906). *Folkways.* Boston, MA: Ginn.

Toale, M. C., & McCroskey, J. C. (2001). Ethnocentrism and trait communication apprehension as predictors of interethnic communication apprehension and use of relational maintenance strategies in interethnic communication. *Communication Quarterly, 49,* 70-83.

Thomas, S. (2007). Outwitting the developed countries? Existential insecurity and the global resurgence of religion. *Journal of International Affairs, 61,* 21-45.

Thiagarajan, S. (2004). *Interactive experiential strategies for multicultural training* (pp. 18-29). Portland, OR: Summer Institute for Intercultural Communication.

Ting-Toomey, S. (1988). Intercultural conflict styles: A face negotiation theory. In Y. Y. Kim & W. B. Gudykunst (Eds.), *Theories in intercultural communication* (pp. 213-238). Newbury Park, CA: Sage.

Ting-Toomey, S. (1993). Communicative resourcefulness: An identity negotiation perspective. In R. Wiseman & J. Koester (Eds.), *Intercultural communication competence* (pp. 72-111). Newbury Park, CA: Sage.

Ting-Toomey, S., Gao, G., Trubisky, P., Yang, Z., Kim, H. S., Lin, S.-L., & Nishida, T. (1991). Culture, face maintenance, and styles of handling interpersonal conflict: A study in five countries. *Journal of Conflict Management, 2,* 275-296.

Ting-Toomey, S., & Oetzel, J. G. (2002). Cross-cultural face concerns and conflict styles. In W. B. Gudykunst & B. Mody (Eds.), *Handbook of international and intercultural communication* (pp. 143-163). Thousand Oaks, CA: Sage.

Ting-Toomey, S., Yee-Jung, K., Shapiro, R., Garcia, W., Wright, T., & Oetzel, J. G. (2000). Cultural/ethnic identity salience and conflict styles. *International Journal of Intercultural Relations, 23*, 47-81.

Todd, A. (2009). From polychronicity to multitasking: The warping of time across disciplinary boundaries. *Anthropology of Work Review, 30*, 49-54.

Tredoux, C., & Finchilescu, G. (2007). The contact hypothesis and intergroup relations 50 years on: Introduction to the special issue. *South African Journal of Psychology, 37*, 667-678.

Triandis, H. C. (1995). *Individualism and collectivism*. Boulder, CO: Westview.

Turner, R. N., & Crisp, R. J. (2010). Imagining intergroup contact reduces implicit prejudice. *The British Journal of Social Psychology, 49*, 129-142.

van de Vijver, F., & Leung, K. (1997). *Methods and data analysis for cross-cultural research*. Thousand Oaks, CA: Sage.

van der Zee, K. I., & Van Oudenhoven, , J. P. (2000). The multicultural personality questionnaire: A multidimensional instrument for multicultural effectiveness. *European Journal of Personality, 14*, 291-309.

Van Lange, P. A. M. (2008). Does empathy trigger only altruistic motivation? How about selflessness or justice? *Emotion, 8*, 766 – 774.

van Oudenhoven, J. P., Mol, S., & van der Zee, K. I. (2003). Study of the adjustment of Western expatriates in Taiwan ROC with the Multicultural Personality Questionnaire. *Asian Journal of Social Psychology, 6*, 159-170.

van Oudenhoven, , J. P., & Van der Zee, K. I. (2002). Predicting multicultural effectiveness of international students: the Multicultural Personality Questionnaire. *International Journal of Intercultural Relations, 26*, 679-694.

Ward, C., & Masgoret, A. M. (2006). An integrative model of attitudes toward immigrants. *International Journal of Intercultural Relations, 30*, 671 – 682.

Weber, R., & Crocker, J. (1983). Cognitive processes in the revision of stereotypic beliefs. *Journal of Personality and Social Psychology, 45*, 961-977.

Weger, H. Jr., Castle, G. R., & Emmett, M. C. (2010). Active listening in peer interviews: The influence of message paraphrasing on perceptions of listening skill. *The International Journal of Listening, 24*, 34 – 49.

Weinreich, P. (2009). 'Enculturation,' not 'acculturation': Conceptualizing and assessing identity processes in migrant communities. *International Journal of Intercultural Relations, 33*, 124-139.

West, R., & Turner, L. H. (2004). *Introducing communication theory: Analysis and application*. New York, NY: McGraw Hill.

Whorf, B. L. (1939). The relation of habitual thought and behavior to language. In J. B. Carroll (Ed.), *Language, thought, and reality: Selected writings of Bejamin Lee Whorf*. Cambridge, MA: MIT Press.

Worchel, S. (2005). Culture's role in conflict and conflict management: Some suggestions, many questions. *International Journal of Intercultural Relations, 29*, 739-757.

Wilmot, W. W., Hocker, J. L. (2007). *Interpersonal Conflict*. New York, NY: McGraw Hill.

Wyer, R. S., Jr., & Gruenfeld, D. H. (1995). Information processing in interpersonal communication. In D. E. Hewes (Ed.), *The cognitive bases of interpersonal communication* (pp. 7-47). Hillsdale, NJ: Erlbaum.

Yoshitake, M. (2002). Anxiety/Uncertainty Management (AUM) theory: A critical examination of an intercultural communication theory. *Intercultural Communication Studies, 11*, 177-193.

Zerubavel, E. (1997). *Social mindscapes: An invitation to cognitive sociology.* Cambridge, MA: Harvard University Press.

Zhang, Q. (2007). Family communication patterns and conflict styles in Chinese parent-child relationships. *Communication Quarterly, 55*, 113-128.

INDEX